Right in the World

Collected Essays

BY GAYLE TROTTER

RIGHT IN THE WORLD
Collected Essays

By Gayle S. Trotter

First Edition April 2022

ISBN 979-8-9855867-0-1

Published in the United States by
American Womens Alliance, LLC

Book Interior and Cover Design by
Cynthia J. Kwitchoff (CJKCREATIVE.COM)

FOR MY FATHER

Hugh A. M. Shafer, Jr.

ABOUT THE AUTHOR

Gayle Trotter is a liberty-loving, tyranny-hating, conservative attorney, political analyst, and columnist with an insider's view of Washington, DC.

She hosts a podcast, ***The Gayle Trotter Show: RIGHT in DC,*** which can be found on her YouTube channel and audio platforms such as SoundCloud, Spotify, iHeart, iTunes, and more.

Gayle is a frequent commentator on *NewsMax, OAN, EWTN,* and *Fox News*. Gayle contributes to *The Hill, The Daily Caller,* and *Townhall,* and appears as a guest on radio shows across the country.

Gayle is a native Washingtonian with conservative political sensibilities that have never lost touch with the heartland of America, and she brings keen insights on the issues of the day and useful connections to power players in our nation's capital.

She attracted national media attention in 2013 with her testimony before the United States Judiciary Committee hearing on gun rights and gun violence in America where she shocked the D.C. establishment by stating that guns make women safer.

Gayle received her BA and JD from the University of Virginia, where she served as an editor of the *Virginia Journal of International Law*, considered among the world's most influential international law journals. She is the cofounder of a law firm in the metro D.C. area that advises entrepreneurs, small businesses, and individuals in business, estate administration, estate planning, taxation, and trust matters.

Her website is www.GayleTrotter.com.

TABLE OF CONTENTS

INTRODUCTION

The fate of unborn millions will now depend, under God, on the courage and conduct of this army.

General George Washington
1776

In January 2010, as President Barack Obama began his second year in office, Americans could see he was not the moderate, post-racial healer of the nation he promised to be on the campaign trail.

Hillary Clinton was his secretary of state, mining her powerful position to enrich herself and her family rather than serving her fellow citizens.

Congress debated the socialized takeover of one-sixth of our economy through Obamacare, which was signed into law on March 21, 2010, and the Islamic State's creation and wanton savagery loomed on the horizon.

What could one person do against the onslaught of a backward "progress"?

I wrote these thoughts, gathered in this book, to help take the fight to socialism, radical Islam, taxation mayhem, and an almost religious assault on our Bill of Rights.

The corporate media continued to do their best to cover up the scandals of the Obama administration, from Operation Fast and Furious to the government-subsidized Solyndra rathole to the IRS's targeting of conservatives and many other scandals of the administration that Barack Obama insisted contained "not a smidgen of corruption." Meanwhile, the same corporate media ceaselessly praised Obama as the messiah (and, no, that is not hyperbole).

In this wilderness of media madness, Americans needed a voice of sanity to cry out. So I did.

I offered my take on what was going on in D.C., from my vantage point right here in the fever swamp, where I am perfectly situated to share my insights with the real America, the one outside the Beltway.

Some of the chapters collected here were previously published in various opinion outlets, including *The Washington Post, The Wall Street Journal, Fox News Online, The Washington Times, Townhall* and *The Daily Caller.* Having reached millions of Americans over the radio and television, I know these are topics that people care about deeply.

In the wake of the horrific school shooting in Newtown, Connecticut, I was asked to testify before the United States Senate Judiciary Committee on the question of what to do about gun violence. I spoke on behalf of millions of American women who know that guns make women safer.

The so-called tolerant left went bananas when I explained how guns are the great equalizer and that gun control laws have a disparate impact on women, the elderly, and the vulnerable. *The New York Times* devoted its lead editorial to lecturing me for my impertinence. In *The Washington Post*, an editorial dismissed me as "phony" for saying, accurately, that millions of American women across the country want their elected representatives to defend women's Second Amendment right to choose to defend ourselves.

When businessman Donald Trump ran in the Republican presidential primary, I covered the many promises he made, including to nominate good judges to the lower federal courts and the Supreme Court. I reported on presidential primary debates and both the Republican and Democrat conventions.

On the night of the 2016 election, I left the downtown television studio where I had provided on-air analysis and ventured over to the White House to soak up the excitement of regime change after eight years of corruption, scandal, and shockingly wrongheaded policy.

I closely covered the Fake Dossier promoted by the Hillary Clinton campaign, amplified by corporate media, and used by the outgoing Obama administration Deep State operatives to try to overturn the election of Donald Trump or to cripple his administration from day one.

I covered the excellent progress made by the Trump administration, including covering the live speech President Trump gave at the March for Life, the first in-person attendance by a president at the march.

When China exported a novel coronavirus worldwide in early 2020, I offered my commentary on the presidential briefings. The pandemic has not changed the mainstream media's war against Donald Trump, I said, but as much as they try to leverage the crisis to debilitate him, their efforts continue to backfire. The president tweeted his personal thanks.

This book contains my thoughts from this important and fractured period of American history. The chapters reflect some of my favorite observations on some key topics most precious to me: American exceptionalism; our Bill of Rights, including the First and Second Amendments; an independent judiciary; corporate media bias; tax policy and entrepreneurship; America-first foreign policy; and, ultimately, the measure of our lives where the most meaning resides, outside of the realm of politics.

President Reagan warned, *"Freedom is a fragile thing and it's never more than one generation away from extinction. It is not ours by way of inheritance; it must be fought for and defended constantly by each generation, for it comes only once to a people. And those in world history who have known freedom and then lost it have never known it again."*

I have fought for and defended our freedom, and I intend to do so until my last breath. Join me in the fight to protect our fragile freedom for this generation and generations to come. The fate of unborn millions will now depend, under God, on the courage and conduct of our fight.

FOREWORD

Let freedom ring. Let us 'highly resolve,' as Lincoln said, that government of the people, for the people, and by the people shall not perish from the Earth. And as for government of the experts, by the experts, and for the experts: No thank you, Dr. Fauci!

This quote from *Right in the World* is a succinct summation of the situation American patriots find themselves in today. As the host of a national radio show called *AMERICA First*, which caters to those who believe that our Republic is the greatest nation on God's green Earth, I have come to the conclusion, after the 2020 election and two years of the China virus, that right now the greatest issue we face as a nation is a collective lack of courage. Gayle Trotter's *Right in the World* is one patriot's timely clarion call.

Courage is the virtue that makes all the other virtues possible. Courage was the indispensable ingredient for our original Revolution, as freedom-loving colonials decided they would take on the greatest empire the world had ever seen because its sovereign had trammeled their "unalienable" rights.

Yet for two years, we seemed to have forgotten the genetic code of our country. Now and again we would hear the story of one restauranteur in California, or a bar owner in New Jersey who refused to comply with unscientific and authoritarian mandates and diktats shuttering private businesses. But these were just outliers. Instead we witnessed the majority of business owners acquiesce, surrendering to unconstitutional orders that robbed them and their employees of being able to provide for and feed their families.

Gayle Trotter is an example of outspoken courage. Whether, for years, as a champion of the Second Amendment, the civil right that makes all other civil rights possible, or when illuminating the responsibility of the Left in helping facilitate the rise of the Jihadi threat, or speaking truthfully on the inestimable damage done to the fabric of the Republic with the Russian "collusion" hoax, Gayle has demonstrated that she is not afraid. We need more Gayle Trotter.

Please read Gayle's book. Buy a copy for a friend. And then be like her.

I ask all my listeners to ask themselves one simple question every day: "What have I done to secure my sacred inheritance as a free person in the greatest nation on Earth?" No nation was founded on the principle of individual liberty based upon our being made in the image of "our Creator," except ours. You have a role in guaranteeing it stays that way.

Sebastian Gorka PhD
Former Strategist to President Trump
Host, *AMERICA First*, SALEM Radio

CHAPTER ONE

The Truth Shall Set Her Free

I BELIEVE HILLARY

The incomparable Michael Kelly wrote one of his most memorable columns on the scandal-ridden administration of President Bill Clinton. I wrote this update to Mr. Kelly's brilliant essay not because I think myself equal to his talents but because his remarks on the Clinton years, updated for today, are as relevant as ever.

I believe Hillary Clinton. I have always believed her. I believed her when she said that her own investment savvy allowed her to realize a 10,000 percent profit by turning a $1,000 investment in cattle futures into nearly $100,000 within ten short months with help from an Arkansas crony, James Blair, just as her attorney general husband was about to become governor. I believed her when she said that Blair did not arrange to have a broker fraudulently assign trades to benefit her account, even though economists calculated the odds of such a return happening as, at best, 1 in 31 trillion.

I believe Mrs. Clinton and her husband did not pressure David Hale, when Bill Clinton was governor of Arkansas, into providing an illegal $300,000 loan to the Clintons' business partner in the infamous Whitewater land deal. I believed Mrs. Clinton when she reported as missing hundreds of pages of her law firm billing records and other documents in response to a grand jury subpoena seeking to investigate the Whitewater matter.

I believe there was nothing ethically suspect about the Whitewater real estate development, for which Mr. Clinton's successor as Arkansas governor, Jim Guy Tucker, was convicted and went to jail for his role in the fraud. I believe that the Clintons had nothing to hide in the matter. I believe that their business partner, Susan McDougal, who served eighteen months in prison for contempt of court for refusing to answer questions about Whitewater and later received a pardon by President Clinton on the very last day of his presidency, was motivated by nothing other than the search for truth.

I believe that it is normal for a First Lady, such as Mrs. Clinton, to become involved in summary firings of longtime White House travel office employees and their replacement with an Arkansas-based travel company with close ties to the Clintons. I believed Mrs. Clinton's view that it was appropriate for friends of the Clintons to become involved in a matter in which they had a business stake. I believed Mrs. Clinton when she said that the report by the Government Accountability Office incorrectly indicated that she played a significant role in the travel office firings, quoting a witness who said she had urged "to get 'our people' into the travel office."

I believe that the White House memo regarding the travel office was misunderstood when it said "there would be hell to pay" unless someone took "swift and decisive action in conformity with the First Lady's wishes." I believe it is typical for a First Lady to take charge of White House personnel matters by firing longtime civil servants and replacing them with campaign hacks. I believe that it was difficult for Mrs. Clinton to remember details of these events in her deposition by the independent counsel reviewing the matter.

I believe it is perfectly plausible that, after nearly two years of searches and subpoenas, a White House staffer "unexpectedly discovered" Mrs. Clinton's long-missing billing records and other documents in the Clintons' private residence in the White House in January 1996, just days after relevant statutes of limitations had elapsed. I believe that personal animus—rather than the evidence surrounding the cattle futures profit, Whitewater and travelgate—motivated *New York Times* columnist William Safire, who had earlier endorsed Mr. Clinton's candidacy, to conclude that Mrs. Clinton is a "congenital liar."

I believe that Mrs. Clinton bears no responsibility for the gross security lapses in Benghazi, Libya that led to the murders of a US ambassador and three other Americans in a terrorist attack while Mrs. Clinton was our nation's top diplomat. I believe it was appropriate for Mrs. Clinton's State Department to blame the incident on a nonexistent protest supposedly fomented by an obscure YouTube video and that Mrs. Clinton rightly refused to acknowledge those attacks, on September 11, 2012, as acts of terrorism. I believe that she aptly bellowed, "What difference at this point does it make?" in response to a senator's question whether "a simple phone call" would have "ascertained immediately that there was no protest."

I believe that Mrs. Clinton's multimillion-dollar tax-exempt organization, the Bill, Hillary & Chelsea Clinton Foundation, is a model of legal compliance and ethical standards. I believe it is appropriate for her foundation to have accepted eye-popping donations from foreign governments despite Mrs. Clinton's calls for campaign finance reform and despite the fact that current law forbids campaign donations from foreign nationals. I believe that major donations to the foundation from countries such as Saudi Arabia, Oman, and the United Arab Emirates were motivated by altruism and, in the foundation's phrase, "the power of creative collaboration."

I believe it was entirely appropriate for Mrs. Clinton to install a private email server in her home to conduct government business as secretary of state. I believe that most high federal government officials have their own private email server at home for use in conducting official federal government business. I believe that Mrs. Clinton permanently deleted from her personal server only "emails about planning Chelsea's wedding or my mother's funeral arrangements, condolence notes to friends as well as yoga routines, family vacations, the other things you typically find in inboxes."

I believe that none of the deleted emails could shed light on any of the dozens of questions about her tenure as secretary of state. I believe that most Americans incorrectly think that Mrs. Clinton purposely deleted or withheld emails relevant to her State Department work.

I believe that *The New York Times, The Los Angeles Times, The Washington Post, Newsweek, Time, US News & World Report, ABC, CBS, NBC, CNN, PBS,* and *NPR* are all part of a vast right-wing conspiracy. Especially *NPR*.

CHAPTER TWO

Hillary Clinton's Supposed Victory Lap

IGNORING BENGHAZI

Hillary Clinton's book, *Hard Choices,* promised readers an "inside account of crises, choices, and challenges" Ms. Clinton encountered as secretary of state, offering Ms. Clinton an opportunity to give a full accounting of flawed decisions and their fatal consequences in Benghazi on September 11, 2012.

That day brought the assassination of US Ambassador Chris Stevens and the murder of three other brave Americans. In an earlier postmortem on those events, Clinton openly asserted that the surrounding circumstances were not relevant to Americans at the time or to determining causes underlying what went wrong.

"What difference at this point does it make?" Clinton indignantly bellowed when Sen. Ron Johnson (R-Wisc.) asked whether "a simple phone call" would have "ascertained immediately that there was no protest."

Johnson pointed out that the American people were told that protests had given rise to the Benghazi assault even though it could have been "easily ascertained that that was not the fact, and the American people could have known that within days and they didn't know that."

The difference this makes is still relevant, and Clinton's question continues to demand an answer. In fact, the causes underlying the slaughter of four Americans makes all the difference in resolving important questions of national security, the safety of our citizens, and the integrity of a national election.

The answers could very well depend on whether the fatal attacks in Benghazi on September 11, 2012 resulted from a protest, the spontaneous actions of "guys out for a walk one night"—a most unlikely scenario that Clinton proposed—or a preplanned attack linked to al-Qaeda.

Decisions matter. In the aftermath of the Benghazi attacks, the Obama administration, the intelligence community, and members of Congress confronted hard choices. Voters expect them to make these tough decisions and to do so competently.

Add to this the irony that Clinton's own 2008 campaign advertisement cited her superior telephonic communication skills as a noteworthy part of her national security prowess. "It's 3 a.m. and your children are safe and asleep," said the narrator, "Who do you want answering the phone?"

The answer matters. For the families of Chris Stevens, Sean Smith, Glen Doherty, and Tyrone Woods, their loved ones were not safe, and the decision makers had the ringer off. Americans were counting on those in charge to take swift and effective action. Washington failed them.

How and why that happened makes all the difference to a nation seeking to understand its leaders' failures.

It makes a difference when a US ambassador's assassins remain at large. It makes a difference when that ambassador is the first killed in over thirty years. It makes a difference when the killers of three other citizens have not been brought to justice. It makes a difference when the Obama administration had failed to provide adequate security even after Ambassador Stevens had reported "unpredictable, volatile and violent" conditions and his repeated calls for increased security went unanswered. It makes a difference when a shameful failure of our national security apparatus emboldens our global enemies. It makes a difference when we project weakness, indecision, and Orwellian dishonesty with our own populace.

It makes a difference when politics trumps safety and security. While Susan Rice toured talk shows insisting that an anti-American demonstration occurred at the Benghazi compound, the CIA already knew the opposite. The administration dissembled over the nature of the Benghazi attacks, but President Obama later insisted just the opposite during the debates, with a transparently biased assist from moderator Candy Crowley.

All of this underscores the latent fiction in Clinton's own 2008 campaign ad. Having claimed to have been better prepared to handle national security matters, her State Department failed to protect Ambassador Stevens and three others, blamed the incident on a non-existent protest supposedly fomented by an obscure YouTube video, and refused to acknowledge the attacks of September 11, 2012 as acts of terrorism.

Clinton or those under her charge could have picked up the phone and determined immediately that no protest had occurred. But when Sen. Johnson pointed this out, Clinton dismissed the question as an absurd irrelevancy.

Clinton campaigned on national security with the ominous question, "Who do you want answering the phone?" Four years later, when pressed to account for actual responsibilities on matters of life and death, Clinton dismissed her interlocutor. Feigning outrage, she posed an equal and opposite question: "What difference at this point does it make?"

At the critical moment of truth, she demonstrated the difference that it makes, but Ms. Clinton never supplied answers rather than just more rhetorical questions. Those who want the nation to entrust them with hard choices should openly discuss the hard facts surrounding past decisions and their consequences. That is something Ms. Clinton has never done.

CHAPTER THREE

Of Emails and Ethics

TECHNICALLY CROOKED

Hillary Clinton's inevitable announcement of her inevitable candidacy has brought inevitable controversy. But history shows that her victory may be anything but inevitable.

Clinton "represents the worst of the Washington machine," said a recent cable TV advertisement. To be sure, she has engaged in a pattern of questionable practices followed by brazen excuses.

In a now-familiar example, Clinton engaged in the unusual practice of using a private email server to conduct government business and has permanently deleted emails that could have shed light on issues now surrounding her campaign, including foreign contributions to her foundation and her role in the Benghazi controversy. Most Americans believe that Clinton purposely deleted or withheld emails relevant to her State Department work, according to a recent Bloomberg poll.

Most telling in the email controversy is the legal argument Clinton deploys in her defense. The reasoning is remarkably similar to an argument that her husband famously used at the time of his impeachment.

Clinton argues that her correspondence would have been captured by government servers because other State Department employees were using government accounts. According to a *Gawker* report, however, at least two other high-level Clinton aides also used personal email accounts, which would mean that communications between Clinton's private email and the aides' private emails would not have been recorded by the State Department.

Let's review Mrs. Clinton's argument. She says that all of her emails touched a government server:

> *"[F]ormer State Department employees, including Clinton's current spokesman Nick Merrill, told* Business Insider's *Hunter Walker that everything about the private account was above board. Two of those employees, Walker writes, argued that "Clinton took care to correspond with other State officials exclusively on their governmental addresses. The officials claimed this meant all of her emails and those sent to her were immediately preserved on government servers."*

This argument may seem vaguely familiar to those who remember the Monica Lewinsky scandal and President Bill Clinton's subsequent impeachment for lying under oath and obstructing justice. At that time, Bill Clinton used similar reasoning to claim that he had not lied under oath.

TIME magazine explained Clinton's argument based on the definition of "sexual relations" used in the deposition in which Clinton committed perjury:

Clinton may have been given the room to offer a technically "true" denial to the question of whether he had sex with Lewinsky—even if she happened to perform fellatio on him. The truncated definition characterizes sex in terms of a checklist of body parts, including the genitals, breast, and thigh. Oral sex would not necessarily require the [p]resident to touch anything on Lewinsky that appears on that list. Strange as it may sound, under one reading of the definition, Lewinsky could have been having sex with him (because she was "touching" the [p]resident's genitals) while at the same moment, he was not having sex with her.

In Hillary Clinton's case, the law says that official emails must be preserved on government servers, and Clinton argues that she complied with this requirement because all of her personal emails involving official business touched a government server.

In Bill Clinton's case, the lawsuit's definition of "sexual relations" referred to any touching of breasts or genitalia, and he argued that his conduct did not implicate the definition because Lewinsky was touching his genitals, but not vice versa.

Hillary Clinton claims her private email server complied with the law because all of her business ended on a government server. Bill Clinton argued that his workplace distractions did not constitute sexual relations because he never touched Lewinsky's business end.

In both cases, the arguments are logically strained, legally specious—and factually fraudulent. Hillary Clinton's email interactions are known to have extended to nongovernmental third parties on official business—such as former Clinton White House adviser Sid Blumenthal on Benghazi-related matters—and Bill Clinton's extracurricular interactions with Lewinsky are known to have extended beyond passively receiving fellatio. And, as a result, Bill Clinton eventually acknowledged perjury and surrendered his law license.

Just as Bill Clinton's political life brought seemingly unending "bimbo eruptions," Hillary Clinton now generates ongoing ethics eruptions. In each case, she and her supporters are quick to offer finely tuned, exotic arguments that hang on strained legal technicalities.

These ethics eruptions, which are frequently tied together in facts and circumstances, promise to challenge the inevitability of a 2016 presidential victory for Hillary Clinton.

She seeks to be the leader of the free world and the commander-in-chief. All she continues to demonstrate is that she is the chief prevaricator. And that's not a role the American people want reprised.

CHAPTER FOUR

Hillary's Fake Dossier

I CALLED IT

From the moment the dossier first became public, it was readily apparent that it was the work product of the Hillary Clinton campaign. As more evidence continues to unfold, we now have proof of what critical observers knew all along.

The thirty-five pages of "salacious" and "unverified" allegations against Donald Trump began, on page 1, with a prominent disclaimer preemptively exonerating Hillary Clinton: "A dossier of compromising material on Hillary Clinton has been collated by the Russian Intelligence Services over many years and mainly comprises bugged conversations she had on various visits to Russia and intercepted phone calls rather than any embarrassing conduct."

For any reader with a reasonable degree of skepticism, the disclaimer was an obvious tell: "The lady doth protest too much, methinks."

First, the disclaimer's prominent placement at the beginning of the dossier would drive home to journalists, politicians and talking heads with similarly short attention spans that—are you sure you're getting this?—Mrs. Clinton engaged in no embarrassing conduct and the Russians have just a few "bugged conversations," that's all.

Second, the tone of the statement is transparently designed to appear evenhanded while in fact exculpating Mrs. Clinton of any wrongdoing. Rather than damning with faint praise, the disclaimer paragraph exonerates with faint criticism: while the Russians intercepted Mrs. Clinton's communications, they found "no embarrassing information." But of course.

Third, there is the substance of the disclaimer paragraph. Even hostile actors who eavesdrop on Mrs. Clinton by intercepting her communications yield only "bugged conversations" and no "embarrassing conduct." Nothing to see here, folks!

The three components of the disclaimer—placement, tone and substance—bore the hallmarks of a carefully scripted public relations ploy. Anyone who was paying attention could see that, and I said so at the time.

As the facts continued to unfold, we saw new revelations of abuse of power, collusion, and foreign conspiracies—and, surprise surprise, the evidence points back to the Clinton campaign.

We know that operatives associated with the Hillary Clinton campaign were feeding information to the author of the Fake Dossier.

New disclosures show how Clinton campaign operatives were involved in funneling information to the Dossier author: a foreign source gave information to a Clinton campaign operative, who in turn gave the information to the State Department, which then gave the information to the dossier author and former British spy Christopher Steele.

In addition to the statement of Rep. Trey Gowdy (R-S.C.), we know that members of the Senate Judiciary Committee recently made a criminal referral to the Department of Justice and the FBI, asking federal law enforcement officials to investigate the dossier author for lying to the FBI, which is a federal crime.

Not only will dossier author Mr. Steele need to answer for a possible federal crime, but the trail of evidence continues to point back to the Clinton campaign and the DNC.

After all, the FBI used opposition research commissioned by one presidential campaign as a justification to spy on the opposing campaign. The FBI had to use the dossier in its FISA application because the FBI lacked enough other evidence to justify surveillance.

To corroborate the dossier, the rabidly anti-Trump Steele and Fusion GPS ginned up breathless fake news stories about the dossier's absurd claims. The FBI did not inform the FISA Court that Mr. Steele ultimately worked for Mrs. Clinton's campaign and the Democratic National Committee.

Months of wiretaps turned up nothing, yet the FBI gave itself open-ended license to spy on a campaign. The FBI subjected Carter Page, a private citizen, to months of government monitoring based on nothing more than gossip from a rival campaign.

All of this is shocking, appalling, and utterly dismaying. And the dossier's provenance was readily apparent from day one to anyone who bothered to look at page one of the dossier.

Liberty is meaningless where the right to utter one's thoughts and opinions has ceased to exist. That, of all rights, is the dread of tyrants. It is the right which they first of all strike down.

Frederick Douglass

CHAPTER FIVE

An Inconvenient Truth

ENHANCED INTERROGATION

The release of a partisan Senate report on the CIA's past interrogation program has renewed the debate over the agency's use of enhanced interrogation methods. These are methods that the Obama administration has often denounced, even while taking credit for killing Osama bin Laden and while continuing the similarly controversial practice of lethal drone strikes.

Controversy surrounds the new Senate report. Critics dismiss it as a partisan hatchet job with a transparent slant and dubious conclusions. Current and former intelligence officials express grave concerns over the security implications of releasing sensitive information that will endanger Americans at home and abroad. Another debate centers on the extent to which enhanced interrogation methods can ever be legally and morally justified, while similar if not identical questions surround the use of lethal drones.

Still another hotly contested question is whether enhanced interrogation methods work. The report claims that the CIA's enhanced interrogations were "not an effective means of obtaining accurate information or gaining detainee cooperation." The issue has obvious relevance to the bin Laden killing.

President Obama touted the killing frequently in his 2012 re-election campaign and since, including in his recent speech promising to "degrade and ultimately destroy" the Islamic State terrorists. He has cited the killing of bin Laden as one of his leading accomplishments.

There are three problems with that. First, it was our nation's intelligence and military personnel who answered the call of duty to gather the intelligence and undertake the mission. "Finding bin Laden was a triumph of bureaucratic intelligence gathering and analysis" that "improved markedly after 9/11 under President Bush," according to Mark Bowden's definitive account on the killing of bin Laden.

Second, "it is difficult to imagine any president of the United States who, under the circumstances, wouldn't have ordered the strike against bin Laden," as P.J. O'Rourke observed. "Although there is Jimmy Carter," Mr. O'Rourke acknowledged. "Thank you for not being Jimmy Carter."

Third, the Obama administration has consistently ignored an inconvenient truth about the mission. The enhanced interrogations that Mr. Obama has so frequently denounced actually yielded important intelligence that helped identify bin Laden's hideout in Abbottabad, Pakistan.

In his book, Mr. Bowden recounts some of the key intelligence gathered using harsh questioning and waterboarding. Coercive methods yielded descriptions of bin Laden's courier from two different al-Qaeda operatives. In addition, Khalid Shaikh Mohammed provided a noteworthy characterization about the courier in "one of his many waterboarding sessions." A fourth source facing harsh methods at a secret

CIA detention center separately corroborated the courier's importance. Tracking the courier led to bin Laden.

"At bottom, we know we got important, even critical intelligence from individuals subjected to these enhanced interrogation techniques," Leon Panetta wrote in his recent memoir. As Mr. Obama's own CIA director at the time of the Abbottabad raid, Mr. Panetta had access to all of the relevant intelligence and understood the years-long, painstaking, and steady accumulation of one lead after another that finally pointed to bin Laden's probable hideout. No single piece of intelligence from any source clinched the matter, but enhanced interrogations provided important pieces of the puzzle.

In particular, Mr. Panetta admits that "harsh interrogation did cause some prisoners to yield to their captors and produced leads that helped our government understand al-Qaeda's organization, methods, and leadership." The former CIA director concedes that harsh techniques often served "precisely" as intended on a prisoner to "break him down and convince him that he has no choice but to cooperate." Mr. Panetta acknowledges that interrogators "extracted" useful intelligence "after unsavory techniques were used."

Those techniques yielded what Mr. Panetta called "critical intelligence" in finding bin Laden, but Mr. Obama seldom misses an opportunity to denounce them. With fanfare and sanctimony, the president in 2009 "rejected the false choice between our security and our ideals" by "banning torture without exception." He recently reiterated that America "tortured some folks" using interrogation methods that "any fair-minded person would believe were torture."

Never mind that the relevant legal question at issue involved a federal statute. Never mind that the so-called torture memos that Mr. Obama controversially declassified contained legal analysis of the statutory provisions. Never mind that those provisions emphatically do not turn on how a fair-minded person would define a vague colloquial term whose commonly understood definition can include anything that might cause mental or physical suffering. Never mind, most of all, that the president's drone strike policy has no better legal or moral footing than enhanced interrogation.

Mr. Obama famously chided America's entrepreneurs not to take credit for their commercial success. "If you've got a business—you didn't build that," he said. "Somebody else made that happen." Yet, in trying to distract from a long list of foreign policy failures, the most significant achievement that the Obama administration claims as its own is the one to which it is least entitled.

CHAPTER SIX

The Truth about a Woman's Right to Choose

SELF-PROTECTION

What should America do about gun violence? That was the question the Senate Judiciary Committee posed for the hearing at which they had asked me to testify.

In my testimony, I explained that the ability to arm oneself is even more important for women than it is for men, since guns level the playing field between women and the physically stronger men who might attack them. We preserve meaningful protection for women by safeguarding our Second Amendment rights to lawful self-protection. I urged the senators to eschew self-defeating proposals that would fail to make Americans safer and would harm women most.

Women often use firearms to defend against violent attacks. For women, guns reverse the balance of power in a violent confrontation because over 90 percent of violent crimes occur without a firearm, according to a federal study.

Concealed-carry laws help reverse that balance of power even before an attack. Criminals cannot tell which potential victims can defend themselves, and armed citizens can better defend against violence. These two effects indirectly benefit unarmed citizens and reduce crime rates, as documented by economist John Lott. The ten states that adopted concealed-carry laws over a fifteen-year span experienced 0.89 shooting deaths and injuries per 100,000 people, less than half the 2.09 per 100,000 experienced in states that did not adopt such laws, Lott found.

My testimony included a detailed summary of twenty-one recent news accounts, each involving a woman using a firearm to protect herself and others against one or more violent men. These examples included a woman who defended herself against five burglars, a woman who thwarted an attempted shooting in a school, a woman who saved her child from a kidnapper, and a woman who stopped a gunman in a movie theater.

Few of these news accounts ever gain national attention, despite their prevalence. Private citizens account for more than one-third of all instances where a violent criminal is killed during the commission of a felony, according to a recent federal study. Americans use firearms defensively 2.2 million to 2.5 million times a year, according to criminologist Gary Kleck, based on a sample in which women represented 46 percent of defensive gun use.

Abundant research has found that reduced gun ownership results in increased criminal home invasions and lethality of attacks on law-abiding citizens. "Homeowners who defend themselves make burglars generally wary of breaking into homes," creating external benefits because "criminals cannot know in advance who is armed," Lott found.

During the Senate hearing, Sen. Chuck Grassley (R-Iowa) asked why a semiautomatic rifle such as an AR-15 has value as a weapon of self-defense. I responded that AR-15 rifles are "accurate, they have good handling, they are light, they are easy for women to hold," and, yes, I highlighted their "scary-looking" appearance. Days later, *The New York Times* cited similar benefits, calling the rifle "fast, modern, ergonomically designed, relatively easy to handle" and highlighting its appearance as "something commandos might carry."

The Supreme Court held in 2008 that the Second Amendment guarantees an individual right to possess a firearm for self-defense and indicated that the right covers weapons "typically possessed by law-abiding citizens"—a standard the AR-15 satisfies, considering that Americans own an estimated 2.4 million to 3.3 million of them. Citizens need not use only "adequate" weapons to protect their families, despite the contrary suggestion of Sen. Sheldon Whitehouse (D-R.I.).

Gun-rights opponents cite debatable or discredited studies claiming private gun ownership does more harm than good. For example, one study by Arthur Kellermann of Emory University asked homicide victims' relatives if the deceased owned a gun in the home. The study gave the misleading impression that the homicide involved the same gun. In fact, of the 444 homicides studied in his paper, only eight deaths involved a gun kept in the home, and Kellerman himself reported that most of the deaths occurred without a firearm. Moreover, Kellermann counted a benefit from defensive gun use only where a criminal had been killed or injured, ignoring the fact that attackers are killed or injured in less than one percent of defensive gun use.

The medical literature on gun control betrays a similar ideological bias. Analyzing research by Kellermann and others, Edgar Suter, a physician, has documented faulty methodologies, false citations, fabricated data, "overt mendacity," and a "failure of peer review." Based on a Harvard study finding that physicians' negligence kills annually three to five times as many Americans as guns, Suter noted the "sad irony" of medical politicians' claim of a "public health emergency" from "guns, rather than medical negligence."

Gun-control measures ignore evidence of civilian gun use and fail to reduce violent crime against women, according to Inge Larish's detailed and scholarly feminist critique of gun control. She found that gun-control measures disproportionately harm women "by restricting or removing the most effective method of self-defense available."

Those who care about women's well-being should work to safeguard our right to keep and bear those types of firearms "typically possessed by law-abiding citizens" to protect ourselves and our families because nearly all violent crimes occur without firearms, making guns the great equalizer for women defending against violent attacks.

CHAPTER SEVEN

Why the Second Amendment Matters

CLINGING TO GUN RIGHTS

"I'm here by myself with my infant," the slight, eighteen-year-old widow told the 911 dispatcher. Two burly men, armed and dangerous, were breaking down the door to her remote rural home.

Sarah McKinley faced impossible odds. The police could not arrive in time to save her. One week earlier, her husband had died of cancer.

The violent intruders wanted McKinley's leftover prescription drugs. One of them was a drug addict.

"It was either going to be him or my son," McKinley later said. "And it wasn't going to be my son."

The men broke down the door, one of them brandishing a foot-long hunting knife.

McKinley fired, averting a tragic ending to a harrowing experience. The other intruder fled.

Guns make women safer. It's an uncomfortable fact for opponents of the Second Amendment. Most violent offenders actually do not use firearms, which makes guns the great equalizer.

Over the most recent decade, from 2001 to 2010, "about 6% to 9% of all violent victimizations were committed with firearms," according to a federal study.

States with nondiscretionary concealed handgun laws have been shown to have 25 percent fewer rapes than states that restrict or forbid women from carrying concealed handguns, as John Lott detailed in his book, *More Guns, Less Crime.*

"There are large drops in overall violent crime, murder, rape, and aggravated assault that begin right after the right-to-carry laws have gone into effect," Lott found. "In all those crime categories, the crime rates consistently stay much lower than they were before the law."

Concealed-carry laws are particularly powerful. For a would-be criminal, they dramatically increase the cost of committing a crime, paying safety dividends even to citizens who do not carry.

Among the ten states that adopted concealed-carry laws over a fifteen-year span, there were 0.89 shooting deaths and injuries per 100,000 people, less than half the 2.09 per 100,000 experienced in states that did not adopt such laws, Lott shows.

Of course, a mass murderer who is bent on slaughtering innocents will find a way to wreak havoc. A teenager in China used a knife in 2012 to kill eight victims and wound five. In 2010, a series of knife attacks in China killed nearly twenty people.

Opponents of the Second Amendment argue that guns increase the death toll in these cases, ignoring the fact that unarmed targets provide less deterrence and only increase the body count.

In recent memory, the US Supreme Court held, in two related 5-to-4 decisions, that the Second Amendment protects an individual's right to possess a firearm for traditionally lawful purposes, such as self-defense within the home.

You would think this was an unremarkable conclusion. For one thing, the constitutional text expressly guarantees the right "to keep and bear arms." For another, the right is specifically enumerated—not implied—and applies to "the people."

In other words, unlike many of the individual rights that the Supreme Court has recognized—some would say invented—you can actually find the right to bear arms in the literal text of the Second Amendment.

The Constitution guarantees a "right of the people" only two other times, both clearly describing individual rights. The First Amendment protects the "right of the people" to assemble and to petition the government, and the Fourth Amendment protects the "right of the people" against "unreasonable searches and seizures."

Even so, the dissenting liberal justices in the Second Amendment cases decried "the Court's announcement of a new constitutional right to own and use firearms for private purposes."

This claim, without a hint of irony, comes from the crowd that finds fundamental individual rights hiding within—I am not making this up —"penumbras" that are "formed by emanations" from "specific guarantees in the Bill of Rights."

The liberal justices maintain that the Bill of Rights generates these "penumbral emanations" from which we get assorted individual rights. But, when the conservatives enforce an individual right actually spelled out in black and white in the letter of the Constitution, the liberals call it the "announcement of a new constitutional right."

Let's see here. Shadowy secretions reveal the hidden meaning of rights secretly embedded in the Constitution and simply awaiting judicial divination, but a specifically enumerated guarantee in the Bill of Rights is "a new constitutional right." Okay, got it.

But that's not all. The liberal justices claimed that it's perfectly fine for a local law to ban private possession of any form of operable firearm because "the adjacent states do permit the use of handguns for target practice, and those states are only a brief subway ride away."

They called this a "minimal burden" on the Second Amendment right to bear arms. Facing down an attacker? Not to worry! Just coax him onto the subway and take a brief ride to the adjoining jurisdiction's nearest target range.

You can bet your bottom dollar that these same liberal justices would take only a few nanoseconds to reject any local law infringing on one of their judicially invented rights—even if "a brief subway ride" would transport aggrieved citizens to another jurisdiction where the penumbral emanations flow freely.

Barack Obama notoriously described "small towns in Pennsylvania" and "small towns in the Midwest" where "bitter" Americans "cling to guns or religion." Since that famously unintended moment of candor, the Supreme Court's liberal justices have shown their similarly elitist outlook on the Second Amendment itself.

We do not elect our federal judges, but we do elect the person who appoints them, and that determines the judicial philosophies of the judges we get.

On the left, we have an approach that routinely invents new rights found nowhere in the Constitution while unapologetically limiting the Second Amendment to protect only the right to have a gun in the army, as bizarre and dangerous as that would be.

On the right, we have an approach that takes seriously the people's enumerated rights—the ones actually written in the Constitution—and respects the Second Amendment.

We continue to face a stark choice between these two alternatives.

CHAPTER EIGHT

Gun-Grabbers Hope You Don't Notice

GUN CONTROL IS SEXIST

Even in the aftermath of unspeakable tragedy like the shootings in Newtown, Conn., gun control zealots advocate mindless and misogynistic policies.

"We have to take action," Vice President Joseph R. Biden Jr. urged in response to the Newtown horror. "The president is absolutely committed to keeping his promise that we will act."

In other words, to quote a frat boy from the movie *Animal House*: "I think that this situation absolutely requires a really futile and stupid gesture be done on somebody's part."

Mr. Biden's statement may sound high-minded in theory, but new gun control efforts will prove ineffective and self-defeating. The Obama administration's proposals will fail to make Americans safer and, worse still, harm women the most.

In reality, guns make women safer. In a violent confrontation, guns reverse the balance of power. Armed with a gun, a woman may even have the advantage over a violent attacker. More than 90 percent of violent crimes occur without a firearm, according to federal statistics. When a violent criminal threatens or attacks a woman, he rarely uses a gun. Attackers use their size and physical strength, preying on women who are at a severe disadvantage.

How do guns give women the advantage? An armed woman does not need superior strength or the proximity of a hand-to-hand struggle. She can protect her children, elderly relatives, herself, or others who are vulnerable to an assailant.

Using a magazine that holds more than ten rounds of ammunition, she has a fighting chance even against multiple attackers. That is, she can protect herself unless she lives in a jurisdiction like the District of Columbia, which criminalizes possession of even an empty magazine that can hold more than ten rounds.

Recently, NBC's David Gregory inadvertently exposed the absurdity of the district's gun laws when he displayed a thirty-round magazine on national television, embroiling himself in a police investigation. Last week, the D.C. attorney general decided not to charge Mr. Gregory. "Despite the clarity of the violation of this important law," he concluded, "a prosecution would not promote public safety." Why is it permissible to possess magazines to persuade people that guns are dangerous, but not for a woman to possess one to defend herself against gang rape?

Armed women benefit even those who choose not to carry. In jurisdictions with concealed-carry laws, women are less likely to be raped, maimed, or murdered than they are in states with stricter gun ownership laws.

All women in these states reap the benefits of concealed-carry laws, which dramatically increase the risk that a would-be assailant faces.

In response to horrific incidents like those in Newtown and Aurora, Colo., politicians advocate more restrictions on gun rights. Hollywood celebrities somberly urge Americans to "demand a plan" to reduce gun violence.

Many of these politicians and celebrities already have a plan: They rely on guns to safeguard their own personal safety. Some critics advocate limiting violence in movies and television, but Hollywood stars apparently do not concur, considering that most of them participate in graphic depictions of lethal violence on the screen.

President Obama said in his first inaugural address, "The question we ask today is not whether our government is too big or too small, but whether it works." Instead of ineffective and self-defeating gestures, we should ask the same question about proposed gun regulations.

Armed security works. That's why snipers stand guard on the White House roof. That's why Sen. Dianne Feinstein, California Democrat and a gun-control advocate, admits to having a gun permit.

Armed guards serve in the employ of the very actors who publicly advocate limiting gun rights. For instance, armed guards protected a suburban newspaper in New York after it published the names and residential addresses of gun permit holders. In fact, the newspaper's own reporter uses a gun for his protection. After publishing the story, the paper's editors disclosed that the reporter "owns a Smith & Wesson 686 .357 Magnum" and has "a residence permit in New York City."

While armed security works, gun bans do not. Anti-gun legislation keeps guns away from the sane and the law-abiding—but it does not keep guns out of the hands of criminals, as the National Rifle Association's Wayne LaPierre has observed. Nearly all mass shootings have occurred in "gun-free" zones. Law-abiding citizens do not bring their guns to gun-free zones, so murderous wackos know they can inflict more harm in these unprotected environments. The sane and the law-abiding become easy targets.

Politicians congratulate themselves for mandating gun-free zones, touting increased safety while actually making us more vulnerable to the next horrible monster in search of soft targets.

If we could simply legislate gun-free zones, why can't our politicians with the stroke of a pen remove all guns from banks, airports, rock concerts, and government buildings?

We already have more than 20,000 under-enforced or selectively enforced gun laws on the books. Gun regulation affects only the guns of the law-abiding. Criminals will not be bound by such gestures, especially as we continually fail to prosecute serious gun violations or provide meaningful and consistent penalties for violent felonies using firearms.

In lieu of empty gestures, we should address gun violence by doing what works. By safeguarding our Second Amendment rights, we preserve meaningful protection for women.

Every woman deserves a fighting chance.

CHAPTER NINE

Limiting Gun Rights Is Step One

OPPRESSION STARTS WITH GUN CONTROL

The White House announced that President Obama is working to adopt executive orders that will unilaterally restrict gun rights. *The New York Times* openly advocated gun confiscation on page one.

The Times urged outlawing civilian ownership of "certain kinds of weapons" and acknowledged, "yes, it would require Americans who own those kinds of weapons to give them up for the good of their fellow citizens."

Americans should consider where this leads. Seventy million mothers, fathers, sons, and daughters died in genocides during the twentieth century. These citizens' governments murdered them after first promulgating so-called gun control regulations that preemptively limited their citizens' right to self-defense.

History teaches that the measures now contemplated by Mr. Obama represent the first step that tyrannical governments take before engaging in campaigns of oppression. For gun-rights proponents, it is no stretch to conclude that Mr. Obama's executive actions are only the first step toward fulfilling the goal of confiscation that *The New York Times* advocated.

At a minimum, you can see why proponents of the Second Amendment have cause for concern. James Madison observed that "the advantage of being armed" is one that "the Americans possess over the people of almost every other nation." Alexander Hamilton wrote that "the best possible security" against a police state is a "large body of citizens" that is "ready to defend their own rights and those of their fellow-citizens."

Mr. Obama wishes to act by fiat to impose new restrictions on gun rights targeting law-abiding citizens.

The Second Amendment is "the Founding Fathers' clear and unmistakable legal statement that an armed citizenry is the bulwark of liberty and provides the fundamental basis for law-abiding Americans to defend themselves, their families, their communities, and their nation against all aggressors, including, ultimately a tyrannical government," according to Jews for the Preservation of Firearms Ownership, an advocacy group.

Time and again, gun confiscation has been the precursor of oppression and genocide. In a legal brief filed with the US Supreme Court in 2008, the JPFO documented this pattern as it has occurred around the world in Ottoman Turkey, the Soviet Union, Nazi Germany and occupied Europe, Nationalist China, Communist China, Guatemala, Uganda, Cambodia, and Rwanda.

The Ottoman Turkish government followed a three-step process to achieve its genocidal aim. First, it enacted Article 166 of the Ottoman Penal Code in 1911, severely restricting the individual right to keep and bear arms. Second, the Turkish government implemented a campaign of gun confiscation from Armenians, sending the Armenians to concentration camps on pain of death for noncompliance. Third, the Turkish government murdered over one million disarmed and defenseless Armenians.

Soviet citizens faced the same three-step process. First, the Bolshevik government implemented a seemingly innocuous regulation requiring universal firearm registration. Second, the government required surrender of individually possessed firearms, except from Communist Party members. Third, the Soviet government murdered tens of millions of its innocent and defenseless civilians.

Nazi Germany implemented the same three steps leading up to the Final Solution. The pre-Nazi government enacted unremarkable firearm licensure requirements and, when the Nazis rose to power, they saw to it that enforcement fell mainly on Jewish citizens. Second, the government implemented systematic firearm confiscation. Third, the Nazi government killed six million Jews.

An armed citizenry can more effectively resist the tyranny of even the most oppressive government. The JPFO recounts how a small number of Jews resisted the Nazi death apparatus for almost a month in the Warsaw Ghetto. Other armed Jews resisted the Nazis in Poland, Lithuania, and Byelorussia, saving innocent lives in the Holocaust. The survival rate of Jewish communities with access to arms was significantly greater than those without arms and rendered defenseless, according to the JPFO's research.

Think this cannot happen in the United States? It already has. Our nation has its own shameful experience of disarming and oppressing an ethnic minority. Slaves in the South faced heavy legal restraints on gun possession and ownership. While armed Northern Blacks successfully faced down angry mobs, Southern Blacks lacked comparable protection.

This system continued after the Civil War freed the slaves, yet Southern state governments acted time and time again to prohibit Blacks from full rights, particularly in the area of gun rights. This practice undergirded the brutal and shameful oppression of Black Americans, including lynchings and Ku Klux Klan intimidation.

The much-ballyhooed example of Australian gun confiscation is inapposite. US citizens own at least one hundred times as many guns as Australians did in 1996, at the time of Australia's confiscation program, and Australia lacks a constitutional guarantee of the "right of the People to keep and bear arms." Madison and Hamilton did not come from the Land Down Under.

With stunning repetition, history shows that gun registration and confiscation represent the initial steps that tyrannical governments implement before undertaking campaigns of complete oppression.

The individual right to keep and bear arms represents the "very last line in the defense of American liberty" and the "final barricade against the unthinkable," as the JFPO has documented. This is a tragically painful lesson that Americans should remember as the Obama administration readies its unilateral assault on the Bill of Rights.

CHAPTER TEN

Protecting Our Children

SCHOOL SECURITY

"How do we protect our children?" NRA president Wayne LaPierre asked Friday morning, the one week anniversary of the horrific mass murders of twenty six- and seven-year-old students and six unarmed adults who died trying to protect them from the murderous rage of a coward.

Parents work to protect their kids almost every waking minute. We feed them healthy food to prevent obesity and illness, we brush their teeth to prevent cavities, we give them mittens and hats to protect them from the cold, we use child seats and seatbelts to make them safer in car rides.

Politicians have touted gun-free zones as another way to protect children and other vulnerable members of society. Gun-free zones actually tell every insane killer in America that schools are the safer place to inflict maximum mayhem with minimum risk, making children easy targets.

Law-abiding citizens respect these laws, but psychopaths know that they are unlikely to face armed resistance if they attack a school.

When guns are wielded by the good guys, guns become the great equalizer for the vulnerable in our society. "The only thing that stops a bad guy with a gun," LaPierre said, "is a good guy with a gun," adding, "Would you rather have your 911 call bring a good guy with a gun from a mile away—or a minute away?"

Already, gun-rights opponents have begun scoffing at the notion of armed guards in our children's schools. That doesn't prevent the gun-rights opponent-in-chief from relying on a government-provided security detail to protect his own children.

On any given school day, no fewer than six marked Secret Service police cars surround the Sidwell Friends School, which the Obama girls attend. In these cars, good guys are ready to respond with deadly force to any threat of harm to the first daughters.

The Secret Service's mere presence deters anyone who would attempt violence at the school founded by Quakers, who adhere to pacifism and nonviolent principles. In this haven of Northwest Washington, D.C., the pacifists depend on guns for protection.

In the same way, citizens of states with concealed-carry laws benefit from lower rates of violent crime. In jurisdictions where law-abiding citizens carry guns, everyone is safer because violent criminals do not know who may or may not be armed. Even those without firearms are less likely to be raped, shot, or murdered.

Those who carry a concealed firearm add a layer of protection for all of us, especially the weakest and most vulnerable.

Parents should demand that communities use the tools we already have available to protect our kids. Armed and trained security guards in every school would assure that all of our kids enjoy a measure of protection similar to what the president rightly provides for his daughters.

Already, the 20,000 different gun laws on the books are not enforced enough, and they certainly did not stop last week's tragedy.

We have armed guards at banks, airports, office buildings, power plants, courthouses, and sports stadiums—but not schools. "How have our nation's priorities gotten so far out of order?" LaPierre asked.

He's right. No one objects to protecting bank lobbies or celebrities. We should all the more protect our most valuable gifts, our children.

We did, after all, form our government to "insure domestic tranquility, provide for the common defense, promote the general welfare, and secure the blessings of liberty to ourselves and our posterity."

If the federal government cannot keep our kids safe, it's simply not doing its job.

And what about other contributing factors to our violent society? Children are not safer from wall-to-wall media coverage of mass murderers. Children are not safer from increasingly gruesome and realistic video games.

Children are not safer from violent movies and television programming. Children are not safer from the lax enforcement of 20,000 gun laws already on the books.

"We must speak for the safety of our nation's children," La Pierre said as he opened his remarks. As a concerned mother, I ask why we need the NRA to speak for our children?

We ask ourselves each day how to protect our children. Banks, airports and rock concerts already know how to do this.

Let's put guns into the hands of trained school guards who can protect our children. No more easy targets.

"Emergencies" have always been the pretext on which the safeguards of individual liberty have been eroded.

FRIEDRICH AUGUST VON HAYEK

CHAPTER ELEVEN

Concealed Carry is the Way

FIGHTING ISIS WITH AN ARMED CITIZENRY

Following the recent Paris attacks, the Islamic State recently announced its intention to "strike America at its center," in Washington, D.C. Our response should be swift and decisive.

The D.C. City Council should immediately adopt emergency legislation to streamline the process for D.C. residents and non-residents who work in or travel to the District to obtain concealed-carry permits for firearms.

Terrorists choose the time and place of their attack. They choose soft targets where they can readily inflict mass casualties. They retain the element of surprise. Unfortunately, there are simply never enough police officers, soldiers or security personnel to safeguard every office building, business, museum, public venue, theater, and residence.

After the *Charlie Hebdo* attack, France dramatically increased security with 10,000 additional soldiers on the street. That did not prevent ISIS from perpetrating a massacre in six Paris locations simultaneously, with 130 dead and 350 wounded.

Soft targets with crowds will always be there. Terrorists will continue to choose soft targets with minimal presence of law enforcement or other security forces. Even where armed security is present—say, at the entrance to an arena or in a restaurant district—terrorists can simply start by killing the armed security personnel or wait for them to leave the area before starting a murderous rampage.

After the recent devastating attack, French President Francois Hollande ordered 1,500 more soldiers into Paris. But given Paris' population of more than 2.2 million people and a geographic area of forty square miles, the addition of 1,500 is a paltry number that will not prevent future attacks.

As economist John Lott suggested shortly after the *Charlie Hebdo* attacks in Paris last January, our leaders need a backup plan to keep us safe.

Concealed-carry laws are a proven strategy that strengthens law-abiding citizens' ability to carry concealed weapons and dramatically increases the terrorists' risk of failure. Currently, D.C. law requires concealed-carry applicants to have completed firearms safety and range training from a certified provider in addition to training in D.C. firearms and self-defense law.

If citizens concealed-carry firearms, potential terrorists lose a key tactical advantage because they are unable to know who might be able to stop them. Even where terrorists intend to select an unsecured target or to begin an attack by neutralizing armed guards or police who are on the scene, the attackers will have no way to predict who or how many private gun owners are in the crowd and ready to respond with deadly self-defense.

The D.C. City Council passed emergency legislation to authorize concealed-carry permits in the district only after a federal court determined that D.C.'s concealed-carry ban violated the constitutional right to bear arms. The court found that D.C. law violated the Second Amendment by imposing unreasonable restrictions on law-abiding citizens who seek to use traditionally permitted firearms for self-defense.

But the council's reflexive overreaction imposed prohibitively onerous regulations. Those restrictions are designed to impede any realistic path for law-abiding citizens to obtain a concealed-carry permit, and they are accomplishing their unfortunate purpose. Since the City Council's measure, D.C. rejected 79 percent of concealed-carry permit applications, according to Lt. Sean Colby, a spokesman for the Metropolitan Police Department, who acknowledged that the department rejected 185 of 233 concealed-carry applications over a one-year period.

ISIS' atrocities in Paris and its own public threats to the district present a new, imminent and urgent threat to the nation's capital. With that threat, the D.C. City Council should again exercise its emergency lawmaking power to change the misguided approach under current law and regulations to ensure that citizens can quickly and easily obtain concealed-carry permits and thereby provide an effective backup plan to help defend against attempted terrorist activities in the city.

These steps could help ensure that so-called soft targets are not actually as soft as they might appear to terrorists. With decisive action, the D.C. City Council could help protect our residents from the threat. The council has the power to act. It should use it.

The people never give up their liberties but under some delusion.

EDMUND BURKE

CHAPTER TWELVE

Speaking Truth on Fighting

MILITANT ISLAM

Somewhere in an alternate universe, White House speechwriters prepared this address for President Obama to deliver to the nation on the Islamic State, also called ISIS. I have no intention of explaining how this document that I now offer to the public fell into my hands—although I note some similarity to the words of Ronald Reagan and Liam Neeson.

My fellow Americans:

At seven o'clock this evening, Eastern Time, air and naval forces of the United States launched a series of strikes against the terrorist facilities and military assets that support the Islamic State. The attacks were concentrated and carefully targeted to minimize casualties among the Iraqi and Syrian people with whom we have no quarrel. From initial reports, our forces have succeeded in their mission.

ISIS is not only an enemy of the United States. Their record of subversion and aggression against innocent people is well-documented and well-known. They have wantonly and indiscriminately raped, murdered, and pillaged. They have committed acts of terrorism in Iraq with a shocking degree of bloodthirstiness.

Today, we have done what we had to do. As necessary, we shall do it again. It gives me no pleasure to say that, and I wish it were otherwise. The people of Iraq are friends of the United States.

I'm sure that most Muslims are ashamed and disgusted that groups such as ISIS have made Islamic jihad a synonym for barbarism around the world. Most Muslim believers are decent people caught in the grip of tyrannical fundamentalists with a history reaching back to the days when Thomas Jefferson sent US Marines to the shores of Tripoli to deal with the Barbary pirates.

Back then, the Tripoli ambassador told Jefferson that, according to the Koran, "all nations which had not acknowledged the Prophet were sinners, whom it was the right and duty of the faithful to plunder and enslave." From the earliest days of our national history, we have boldly confronted the double threat of tyranny and state-sponsored religion. We were not fooled then, and we are not fooled now.

We Americans are slow to anger. We always seek peaceful avenues before resorting to the use of force—and we did. We have tried quiet diplomacy, public condemnation, economic sanctions, and demonstrations of military force. None succeeded. Despite our repeated warnings, ISIS has continued its grotesque acts of savagery, intimidation, and relentless pursuit of terror.

Finally, I also have a message for those members of the Islamic State directly involved in the kidnapping and beheading of our citizens, James Foley and Steven Sotloff. At this point, I don't know who you are. I don't know what you expect to accomplish. If you are looking for the United States to abandon its resolve, I can tell you we don't have that in our nature.

What we do have is a very particular set of skills, skills we have acquired over a very long history of leading in world affairs. Skills that make us a nightmare for people like you. We will look for you, we will find you, and we will kill you. And we will accord the same treatment for your accomplices and your affiliates.

ISIS has made the first of several fatal miscalculations. They counted on America to be passive. They counted wrong.

I am proud to be the commander-in-chief of the soldiers, sailors, airmen, and Marines who are risking their lives to help ensure our safety. They and the men and women of our Foreign Service and intelligence community continue to serve with distinction. They have my gratitude and, I'm sure, the gratitude of all Americans.

We are sending a message to terrorists everywhere. The message: You can run, but you can't hide.

I warned that there should be no place on Earth where terrorists can rest and train and practice their deadly skills. I meant it. I said that we would act with others if possible, and alone if necessary, to ensure that terrorists have no sanctuary anywhere. Tonight, we have.

Thank you, and may God continue to bless the United States of America.

For with what judgment ye judge, ye shall be judged; and with what measure ye mete, it shall be measured to you again.

MATTHEW 7:2

CHAPTER THIRTEEN

The Measure of All Things

MEASURING YOUR LIFE

Clayton Christensen, the late Harvard Business School professor, once asked in the *Harvard Business Review*, "How will you measure your life?" (Tagline: *"Don't reserve your best business thinking for your career."*)

We all have different ways of measuring our lives and the lives of those around us, for better and for worse. For some, this quest for meaning centers on the pursuit of happiness, while for others it might mean perfecting their bodies in search of fame and fortune.

To this variety of approaches, Christensen adds his own life experiences and professional expertise. In his HBS classes, Christensen focuses on teaching models of effective business management theory and how the theory is built. After the students learn the model, they have an analytical framework rather than a set of bottom-line answers. In other words, they learn how to think, not what to think. Christensen uses this same approach when he counsels major corporations and their CEOs on how to analyze the challenges their businesses face.

On the last session of his HBS class, Christensen would ask his students to turn their newly developed analytical skills back on themselves and answer three crucial questions, using his own life as a case study for evaluating the questions as they begin their careers.

(1) How can you be sure you will be happy in your career?

This question is particularly relevant to the MBA class of 2010, which entered business school in the fall of 2008 with a strong economy and endless possibilities only to find themselves facing a poor economy, more limited prospects upon graduation, and, for some, massive tuition debt.

Softening this blow, Christensen recalled Frederick Herzberg's argument that money is not the prime motivator, as opposed to the "opportunity to learn, grow in responsibilities, contribute to others, and be recognized for achievements." Although he gives no specific answer to the question, he calls them to reflect on what their prime motivator may be, suggesting that they should pursue careers with the characteristics that Herzberg identified rather than merely the greatest income potential.

(2) How can you be sure that your relationships with your spouse and family become an enduring source of happiness?

To answer this question, Christensen recommends creating a strategy for your life. You must initially define your strategy and then decide how to implement it. Proper resource allocation undergirds implementation of a successful strategy. For example, businesses frequently make the mistake of funding investments that yield tangible results and immediate returns. Similarly, as an example of personal resource misallocation, Christensen cites his experience attending his HBS Class of 1979 reunions and noticing that more and more of his classmates return to reunions "unhappy, divorced, and alienated from their children."

He points out that not a single one of his classmates set out with the "deliberate strategy of getting divorced and raising children who would become estranged from them," and yet a larger-than-expected number implemented just that failing strategy.

He urges his students to reflect now on their purpose in life because, for most young professionals, life becomes only more demanding as their careers progress and their personal lives include children and mortgages. As an example, Christensen describes how he discovered his purpose in life while on a Rhodes Scholarship at Oxford. Despite a potentially all-consuming academic load, Christensen devoted an hour each day to reading, thinking, and praying about "why God put me on this earth." Although he could have allocated that hour to studying his chosen field, he reasoned that he would apply his knowledge of his life's purpose every day and that it would be a rudder in the rough seas of his life. "Without a purpose," he cautioned, "life can become hollow." If your purpose is financial success, where does that leave you when the bottom falls out?

Christensen highlights time, energy, and talent as the personal resources we have to ensure that our relationships will provide enduring happiness. Each of us has several personal enterprises, which may include our spouse, kids, community, career, and church. High achievers allocating resources, whether it be an extra half hour or an extra bit of energy, tend to direct those resources to endeavors that return the most immediately recognizable achievements. Contrast that paradigm with the business of raising children. "Kids misbehave every day," Christensen points out, and it is "not until twenty years down the road that you can put your hands on your hips and say, 'I raised a good son or daughter.'" The result of this dichotomy? "People who are driven to excel have this unconscious propensity to underinvest in their families and overinvest in their careers—even though intimate and loving relationships with their families are the most powerful and enduring source of happiness."

In further addressing the second question, Christensen outlines a model called the Tools of Cooperation. The model explains how to create cooperation among constituents of an organization to propel the organization forward. Initially, "power tools," such as coercion, threats, and punishment, are used until a culture of cooperation is built. Parents likewise start raising children by using power tools while simultaneously creating a family culture. If the family culture is respectful, then the parents can rely on the culture they have created when their kids hit the teen years and power tools no longer suffice. Families have cultures, and we can be deliberate in the creation of these cultures for the benefit of each family member.

(3) How can you be sure you will stay out of jail?

This final question is neither frivolous nor academic. Shocking as it may be to ask a group of highly driven HBS overachievers how they plan to stay out of jail, Christensen notes that two out of his thirty-two fellow Rhodes Scholar classmates spent time in jail and that Enron's Jeff Skilling was an HBS classmate.

Christensen then shows how the model of "avoiding the 'marginal costs' mistake can apply to answering the third question." In particular, rather than calculate the full cost of wrong behavior and where it eventually takes us, "we use the alluringly low 'marginal cost' of the action 'just this once.'" The "marginal cost economics of 'just this once'" provides "justification for infidelity and dishonesty in all their manifestations." Christensen recalls a moment in his life when he realized that it is "easier to hold to your principles 100% of the time than it is to hold to them 98% of the time." Like Eric Liddell in *Chariots of Fire*, Christensen had to choose whether to adhere to a lifelong vow not to play basketball on Sunday or to disappoint his teammates in their championship collegiate basketball game. Christensen declined to play and found that his decision strengthened his resolve to adhere to that principle throughout the rest of his life. The point, of course, is about staying true to your principles and honoring your word, not simply the propriety of Sunday basketball.

Christensen also admonishes his students to remember the importance of humility. Humble people possess high self-esteem. After his students graduate from HBS, Christensen surmises that most of the people they will daily interact with may not be smarter than them, unlike their experience over the course of their educational careers. He cautions, "if your attitude is that only smarter people have something to teach you, your leaning opportunities will be very limited." People who believe they are always the smartest guys in the room are bound to regret it.

Ultimately, Christensen counsels that you "think about the metric by which your life will be judged, and make a resolution to live every day so that in the end, your life will be judged a success." In the end, he provides an analytical framework for accomplishing this objective, rather than a list of action items.

The bottom line: consider your metric and make it guide your daily living, even in the smallest decisions.

The power to tax involves the power to destroy.

CHIEF JUSTICE JOHN MARSHALL

CHAPTER FOURTEEN

Obamacare and the Supreme Court

WHAT'S AT STAKE

When the Supreme Court first heard arguments in 2012 on whether Obamacare exceeded the federal government's power under the US Constitution, many observers pointed out that the federal government had never before in the 220-year history of the Republic forced citizens to buy a product.

That all changed with Obamacare. No federal law had ever before exercised such extravagant power over the individual choices of every man, woman, and child. But the Patient Protection and Affordable Care Act of 2010, more commonly known as Obamacare, does exactly that.

Obamacare requires almost everyone living in the United States to purchase health insurance. The provision that does this is euphemistically called the "individual mandate." The Obama administration argued that a "compelling" federal interest in health care justifies this power grab.

Next up: compulsory purchase of broccoli and gym club memberships. After all, healthy eating and fitness directly affect the health of our citizenry and, with it, the cost of health care.

If the Constitution authorizes the federal government to compel every citizen to buy health insurance—whether they want it or not—the same logic would justify federally mandated veggies and exercise.

Under the original statute, violators of the individual mandate would pay a hefty financial penalty. This may sound like a tax, but Obama has adamantly insisted that the "penalty" is not a tax.

"For us to say you have to take responsibility to get health insurance is absolutely not a tax increase," he said in 2009, while arguing for the law's passage. "Nobody considers that a tax increase."

Except the administration's lawyers. Now that they are defending the law in court, they argue that Obamacare is constitutional precisely because it's a tax increase.

Got that? It's not a tax when you're trying to sell the proposed legislation to the public. But when you need the law to survive a court challenge, well, of course it's a tax.

Our founders designed our federal system to make it difficult to pass new laws. They did this to ensure that voters would hold lawmakers accountable.

This is especially so with taxes. "The power to tax involves the power to destroy," Chief Justice John Marshall famously wrote.

The Obama administration wants to have it both ways. If you're a voter, please don't think of the individual mandate as a tax. If you're a Supreme Court justice, of course it's a tax!

This is nothing new. During the New Deal era, the Roosevelt administration faced a similar problem in getting the Social Security Act passed and upheld in court.

Roosevelt's secretary of labor, Frances Perkins, could not figure out how to stretch the federal government's power further than ever before. Then she got a hot tip at a D.C. cocktail party.

Perkins could not invent a constitutional basis for the massive expansion of federal power known as Social Security. Then she had an experience that, today, we would call a classic inside-the-Beltway moment.

On a social visit to Justice Harlan Stone's house, Perkins chatted privately with him, lamenting her difficulties in finding a constitutional hook for the Social Security Act.

"We are having big troubles," she said to Justice Stone. She was "not quite sure, you know," how to keep the law from being overruled as unconstitutional.

Justice Stone "looked around to see if anyone was listening," Perkins later recounted. Then he put his hand up, whispering confidentially, "The taxing power, my dear, the taxing power." Then he added, "You can do anything under the taxing power.'"

"I didn't question him any further," Perkins said. "I went back to my committee and I never told them how I got my great information. As far as they knew, I went out into the wilderness and had a vision."

Supreme Court justices are not permitted to give advisory opinions. The Constitution requires justices to decide actual cases and controversies. Moreover, the executive branch and judicial branch are supposed to be separate.

None of those pesky facts got in the way of Justice Stone's legal advice to Secretary Perkins. That's why Stone gave the advice confidentially, in a hushed whisper. That's why Perkins never revealed her source until long after the Supreme Court had upheld the Social Security statute.

Later she would proudly proclaim, "Social Security is so firmly embedded in the American psychology today that no politician, no political party, no political group could possibly destroy this Act and still maintain our democratic system."

That's what happens after the Supreme Court upholds a massive entitlement program. It never goes away. It never can.

And that's what was at stake when the Supreme Court considered the validity of Obamacare. Does the federal government have this much power?

If not, the statute must fail. The federal government's powers are "enumerated"—specifically listed—in the Constitution. The federal government can regulate commerce, but that has never before meant compelling citizens to purchase something or punishing inactivity—not purchasing insurance.

As I predicted at the time, if the Court upholds Obamacare, we know from experience that the statute will never go away. No politician, no political party, no political group could possibly repeal it and still maintain our democratic system.

Frances Perkins taught us that.

CHAPTER FIFTEEN

Supreme Court Grabs

TAXING POWER

Multiple days of Supreme Court arguments in the Obamacare case laid bare the Obama administration's incoherent defense of its signature legislation.

To this day, Obamacare, officially called the Patient Protection and Affordable Care Act, represents an extravagant exercise of federal power over the individual choices of every man, woman, and child.

For the first time in the history of the Republic, federal law required virtually every American citizen to purchase a product. Those who do not must pay money to the federal government.

Today, the mandatory product is health insurance. Tomorrow, look for purchase mandates for electronic cars, solar panels, soybean burgers, vegetables, or whatever the nanny state wants you to do.

When the law forces law-abiding citizens to pay money to the government, we call the payment a tax. When citizens must pay money for violating the law, we call it a penalty or a fine.

Obamacare mandates a payment to the government by those who violate the requirement to buy health insurance. Is that a tax or a penalty?

"I can make a firm pledge," Obama repeatedly and emphatically promised, "no family making less than $250,000 a year will see any form of tax increase." Obama said his no-new-taxes guarantee encompassed all forms of taxation: "Not your income tax, not your payroll tax, not your capital gains taxes, not any of your taxes."

When the Obamacare bill gained momentum in Congress, observers noted that the law imposed a massive tax increase on the very people Obama promised not to tax.

Responding to this charge, Obama said that the mandatory payment is "absolutely not a tax increase." He and the other proponents of the legislation, which squeaked through the House of Representatives by a margin of just seven votes, sold the law to the American people saying that it was not a tax.

Then, as I wrote in April, the Obama administration shamelessly argued that the Supreme Court needed to uphold Obamacare because it was a tax.

Got that? When you're selling the law to the American people, it's "absolutely" not a tax. When you're selling the law to five unelected, life-tenured lawyers in robes—it's most emphatically a tax. The people can have their tax and eat it too.

Court-watchers all thought the tax argument was a long shot.

For one thing, not a single lower court had found that the federal taxing power authorized Congress to impose Obamacare's mandate for everyone to buy health insurance.

For another thing, federal law requires taxpayers to pay a tax before they can legally challenge it in court, and Obamacare's purchase mandate does not kick in for another two years.

Plus, Obama and many others in the administration had said ad nauseam that the Obamacare payment is not a tax. You would think that federal officials who are taking money out of people's pockets should own up to what they are doing.

No such luck. The administration and its lawyers had been reading their Emerson: "Speak what you think now in hard words, and tomorrow speak what tomorrow thinks in hard words again, though it contradict everything you said today."

That's nice personal advice from a pep talk about self-reliance. But it leaves something to be desired when applied to a government of laws, and not of men.

It's one thing for a politician to take logically incoherent positions. It's quite another for the Supreme Court to do so. Least of all did anyone expect that from Chief Justice Roberts.

One of the chief justice's law professor defenders called his reasoning "legally incoherent all over the place but strategically brilliant." Last I checked, we don't ask our judges to be strategic thinkers. Legal coherence would be just fine, thank you.

Roberts flatly rejected the administration's arguments that the federal commerce power authorized Congress to enact Obamacare. His passionate defense of limited government and federalism would have made James Madison and Alexander Hamilton proud. Roberts spoke gravely of "the country the Framers of our Constitution envisioned."

After this solemn description of the Framers' vision for our country, Roberts turned tail and ran directly in the opposite direction. Conceding that "the statute reads more naturally as a command to buy insurance than as a tax," he proceeded to conclude that Obamacare's purchase mandate is indeed a tax and therefore hunky dory.

"Because the Constitution permits such a tax," Roberts said, "it is not our role to forbid it, or to pass upon its wisdom or fairness." In other words: don't blame me, blame any seven congressmen who could have voted against Obamacare but didn't.

That's just the beginning of the incoherence. Remember that federal law prevents any court—even the Supreme Court—from hearing a tax challenge until after a person pays the tax. Yet the individual mandate does not take effect until 2014.

So how could the mandate survive as a tax? If the mandate is a tax then the Supreme Court did not even have authority to hear the case.

Roberts decided that the mandate is not—repeat not—a tax under the statute that says people cannot challenge a federal tax law until they have already paid the tax. He concluded that Obamacare does not impose a tax because the statute does not call the mandate a tax.

"Congress," Roberts said, "chose to describe the 'shared responsibility payment' (or individual mandate) imposed on those who forgo health insurance not as a 'tax,' but as a 'penalty.'"

Wait a second. To uphold the mandate as a valid exercise of the taxing power, Roberts had to determine that the payment actually is a tax.

As far as Roberts is concerned, the individual mandate can be whatever it needs to be. When the mandate needs to be a "penalty" to fall outside of the statute that prohibited the Court from hearing a tax case, then it's not a tax. When the mandate needs to be a "tax" to fall within the federal taxing power, well of course it's a tax.

The four conservatives denounced Roberts's magic trick. "That carries verbal wizardry too far," they said, "deep into the forbidden land of the sophists."

In the preceding chapter, I described how Justice Harlan Stone—through an inappropriate advisory opinion—gave Franklin Roosevelt's labor secretary, Frances Perkins, the winning design for structuring Social Security so that the Supreme Court would uphold it.

"You can do anything under the taxing power," Stone whispered to Perkins at a cocktail party. And yet, as broad as Stone's claim may sound, it was too modest.

As it turns out, Congress can now do anything, period. It can take over a sixth of the national economy and require all citizens to purchase health insurance.

It doesn't matter if the president insists that the legislation is not a tax. It doesn't matter if the statutory text says it's not a tax.

Even if Congress doesn't use the taxing power, the Supreme Court will.

No legislative act contrary to the Constitution can be valid.

Alexander Hamilton
Federalist No. 78

CHAPTER SIXTEEN

Naked Power and the Supreme Court's

COMPROMISED LOGIC

Was there anything interesting in *Time* magazine's fawning coverage of the chief justice's Obamacare decision? Oh yes. The twenty fourth paragraph.

"It's hard to believe, but generations of Americans considered compromise an admirable quality," David Von Drehle argued as he concluded his analysis. "Now," he lamented, "the word connotes something bad."

After all, he claims, the Great Compromise and the Missouri Compromise demonstrate prior generations' long-standing esteem for compromise. He contrasts that with today's supposedly compromise-hating culture, in which "a leaky gasket has been 'compromised,' and cheating spouses are caught in 'compromising' positions."

It's a nice theory, but total nonsense. The word "compromise" and its derivations have had both good and bad connotations for over 400 years, meaning "expose to risk or censure" as well as "damaged or discredited." Thomas Jefferson used the word in its negative sense in 1785, and it was hardly new then, considering that Shakespeare had done the same thing almost 200 years earlier.

You have to wonder why *Time's* cover story on the Obamacare decision would resort to spurious word history to advance a dubious socio-political critique. It's as if they just make this stuff up as they go along.

Time lavishly praised Roberts for standing "above the viral, toxic cloud of partisan rancor" and establishing himself as "perhaps the healthiest figure, politically speaking, in government."

Of course, *Time's* Von Drehle would scarcely have extolled the brilliance of the resulting "compromise" if the Supreme Court had decided 5-to-4 to strike down the individual mandate or, better yet, the whole statutory mess.

All of which is beside the point. The court's decision to uphold Obamacare was not a compromise in the first place. It was a total defeat of conservative jurisprudence. For the first time in over two centuries, the Supreme Court permitted the federal government to force citizens to buy a product.

The result is bad enough, but the reasoning is an illogical muddle.

Roberts says, in effect, that the Founding Fathers would roll over in their graves if Congress used the federal commerce power to force citizens to buy a product, and then he says Congress can get to the same place as long as they use the taxing power to do it.

Roberts concedes that "the statute reads more naturally as a command to buy insurance than as a tax" but stretches to uphold the mandate as a tax even though he has to find that Congress did not intend to invoke the taxing power as a prerequisite for the Supreme Court to hear the case under the Anti-Injunction Act.

"It is not our job to protect the people from the consequences of their political choices," Roberts says.

Nor is it the Supreme Court's job to make political compromises.

Instead, the justices are supposed to apply "neutral principles" that transcend any immediate result and provide a reasoned analysis derived from the Constitution. When the court fails to decide a constitutional issue in a principled way, it simply functions as a "naked power organ," as a court watcher famously said.

"Roberts brought the court down squarely on the side of one of the most basic conservative principles of all," Von Drehle contends, "that big decisions in the US should be made not by judges or bureaucrats but by voters."

Wrong again. In reality, Roberts's failure to abide by this principle is exactly why his ruling has thoroughly disgusted conservatives.

He rewrote the statute's penalty as a tax, contrary to the Obama administration's long-standing characterization of the law, the statutory text, and Roberts's own conclusion on the question in the first part of his own opinion.

As a result, the federal government could enact an unpopular law without having to call it a tax. Had proponents conceded that it was a tax, the law never would have passed, and Obama would have had to explain to voters why his plan violated his no-new-taxes pledge to families earning less than $250,000.

Moreover, whether judges get to make a "big decision" depends on what the decision involves. The legislature cannot contradict the Constitution.

"No legislative act contrary to the Constitution can be valid," Hamilton wrote in *Federalist No. 78*, explaining the basis of judicial review. This was a full year before the states had ratified the Constitution and several years before Chief Justice John Marshall's famous opinion in *Marbury v. Madison*, marking the Supreme Court's first instance of setting aside a federal statute as unconstitutional.

Two centuries later, President Obama warned the Supreme Court justices against taking "an unprecedented extraordinary step of overturning a law that was passed by a strong majority of a democratically elected Congress."

In a sense, Obama was correct. That is, if "unprecedented" means "originally conceived before ratification of the Constitution and routinely exercised since 1803" and if "strong majority" means seven representatives in Congress.

But the Founding Fathers had an altogether different notion of judicial review. The Federalist Papers clearly explain why judges can declare laws unconstitutional: "where the will of the legislature, declared in its statutes, stands in opposition to that of the people, declared in the Constitution, the judges ought to be governed by the latter rather than the former."

Congress adopted Obamacare. "We the People" adopted the Constitution. The judiciary should have been governed by the latter rather than the former.

CHAPTER SEVENTEEN

Guy Who Never Ran a Business Lectures Job Creators

YOU DIDN'T BUILD THAT

"If you've got a business—you didn't build that," President Obama told supporters in Roanoke, Virginia on July 13, 2012. "Somebody else made that happen."

Last I checked, it was the other way around. If you're running the federal government—you didn't build that.

Predictably enough, Obama quickly backpedaled from the inadvertently transparent insight he provided into his administration's real ideology—one that so many Americans find antithetical to our country's founding principles. "What I said," he later claimed, is that "together we build roads and we build bridges."

Of course, if that were true, none of this would have made news in the first place. "News flash: Roads and bridges built by government, not entrepreneurs."

Taxpayers paid Obama's $400,000 annual salary. Roads, the Internet, and everything that Obama says "somebody else made" were financed by American taxpayers, including businesses from sole proprietors mowing lawns to employees of medium-sized businesses to those on the Fortune 500 list.

To be sure, government adds value. Maintaining law and order, providing a military, and securing "the Blessings of Liberty for ourselves and our Posterity," to name a few.

But government cannot create wealth. Government revenue comes from Americans' toil and sweat, and recently, big IOUs to foreign countries with awful human rights violations and global ambitions.

Obama invoked firefighters and teachers in his Virginia speech, but not Solyndra. We could use more public safety personnel and educators. Too seldom do taxpayer funds go toward hiring more of the workers that we need. Too often the money goes down a rathole like Solyndra and so many other programs.

"There are a lot of wealthy, successful Americans who agree with me," Obama said, "because they want to give something back." Great, let those "wealthy, successful Americans" give whatever they want to the federal government, but please keep your hands off the paychecks of ordinary hardworking citizens.

Let's not kid ourselves that the federal tax code has anything to do with "giving." A gift does not land you in legal jeopardy when you decline to give it.

Business owners want to give back to their families, their customers, and their communities. A landscaping company takes care of the community little league fields, just because it can. Giving back is not the same as paying taxes on threat of jail for noncompliance.

When a reporter posed the immediate opportunity to "give back" to the US Treasury, famous liberals refused the opportunity.

Truly "giving back" means spending more time with family and volunteering with the community. Think of the volunteer hours that are lost each year when Americans have to spend so much time keeping in compliance with the regulatory state and working longer hours to pay taxes to a government that spends recklessly while telling Americans that they aren't being prudent enough.

If business owners can't claim success for their businesses, how can the administration claim success for anything it has done? The business owners are at least the proximate cause of their own success. If they didn't choose to get out of bed each morning, there would be no business.

"You're still betting on hope and you're still betting on change," Obama importuned, "and I am still betting on you." That's all we have left at this point. A hope and a prayer. A moonshot wager.

Betting is the opposite of building. Building is time-consuming, creative, and inspiring to others around you.

Betting is the language of something for nothing. Betting is for an easy payout instead of years of hard work.

Obama repeatedly invokes the "bargain" instead of the American Dream. "But what we also understood was that we weren't going to stop," Obama promised, "until we had restored that basic American bargain that makes us the greatest country on Earth."

The American bargain? The American dream has become the American bargain.

"Maybe you can take a little vacation with your family once in a while" Obama proposed, "nothing fancy, but just time to spend with those you love." If you vote for him, he will be sure you can take a vacation once in a while.

Not jet-setting to exotic locales at taxpayer expense, but "maybe see the country a little bit, maybe come down to Roanoke."

Obama had the idea of government completely wrong. "The basic bargain" that Obama claims as having "built this country" was no bargain.

Obama was right in one respect though: "What's at stake is a decision between two fundamentally different views about where we take the country right now."

No longer the post-racial healer, the unifier, the advocate of the underdog. Obama's Roanoke remarks exposed him as a card-carrying member of the jet-setting liberal class that wants to bargain with the American people to win their votes.

CHAPTER EIGHTEEN

Regulation Run Amok

FOOD FREEDOM

Episode 115 of *Seinfeld* featured a gruff entrepreneur who ran a soup stand offering the best soup in New York City. "You can't eat this soup standing up, your knees buckle," Jerry Seinfeld explained to Elaine.

"There's only one caveat—the guy who runs the place is a little temperamental, especially about the ordering procedure," Jerry said. "He's secretly referred to as the Soup Nazi" because if you don't order right, "He yells and you don't get your soup."

No one liked the Soup Nazi—but everyone loved his soup! Despite his grumpy, rude, and domineering demeanor, the Soup Nazi's recipes would command long lines out the door of his shop because he offered irresistibly delicious food at a reasonable price.

The Soup Nazi freely chose what to serve and how to serve it. His customers voted with their taste buds. Good cooking trumped bad manners.

Life imitated art in a San Francisco restaurant whose owner lost it in response to customers who could not order right. James Chu's restaurant offered old-fashioned, conventional fare, and he got "fed up with trying to satisfy every single patron's particular demands."

The last straw was a customer who said, "The rule is, if we don't like it we don't have to pay," and then walked out cursing. "That's when I went poof," said Chu.

Chu temporarily closed the restaurant, posting a sign: "So, yes we use MSG! So, we don't believe in organic food. And, we don't give a s--- about gluten free." There, he said it.

Instead of genuflecting to free-range, fair-trade, cruelty-free, wind-powered, non-GMO, non-transfat, gluten-free, no-MSG, crunchy-granola organic chicken, Chu cries conventional fowl. Soup Nazi and Joe the Plumber, meet James Chu, entrepreneur for sanity.

Chu personifies the last vestige of the free-market economy in America. It's a refreshing change to see that a shred of freedom remains in a world where agents shut down a child's lemonade stand for lack of a business license, where local governments ban transfats and salts, where New York City bans large sodas, where state governments dictate the wages entrepreneurs must pay their employees, where Michelle Obama decrees "Let them not eat cake" at elementary school fundraisers, where government regulation runs amok and small businesses face seemingly endless job-killing bureaucratic red tape.

It is easy to imagine nanny-state bureaucrats and politicians imposing their own views on Chu and other entrepreneurs. For now, we can celebrate Chu's freedom to serve Chinese food that contains (gasp!) MSG and gluten, and we thank him for showing that, for now, the idea of America is not yet dead.

"It is not from the benevolence of the butcher, the brewer, or the baker that we expect our dinner, but from their regard to their own interest," wrote Adam Smith. "We address ourselves, not to their humanity but to their self-love, and never talk to them of our own necessities but of their advantages." If Chu's customers demand MSG-free Chinese food, he can give them what they want or go out of business. But if they want MSG in their kung pao chicken, Chu is free to serve it up.

That, after all, is what the free market is all about. Entrepreneurs choose what they sell. Customers vote with their taste buds, their pocketbooks, and, ultimately, their feet. We don't need government dictating what the result will be.

Our local, state, and federal government has decided that food is the new sex, as Mary Eberstadt has argued. "The rules being drawn around food receive some force from the fact that people are uncomfortable with how far the sexual revolution has gone—and not knowing what to do about it, they turn for increasing consolation to mining morality out of what they eat."

The hyper-regulation of food and entrepreneurs borders on obsession, with an effectiveness that exceeds that of the Puritans. But James Chu reminds us that we generally don't need laws to make choices that market forces can make on their own.

"We work hard to please everyone, but we know we can't," reads Chu's newest sign. "So if you're hard to please, please just turn around and go somewhere else. Thanks!" On that day, San Francisco retained a morsel of freedom, even if only for a fleeting moment.

As a child in the Deep South, I'd grown up fearing the lynch mobs of the Ku Klux Klan; as an adult, I was starting to wonder if I'd been afraid of the wrong white people all along.
My worst fears had come to pass not in Georgia, but in Washington, D.C., where I was being pursued not by bigots in white robes, but by left-wing zealots draped in flowing sanctimony.

JUSTICE CLARENCE THOMAS

CHAPTER NINETEEN

Barron's AP Test Prep Guide Reveals

CRAZY-LIBERAL BIAS

Those who track partisan tendencies in academia can mark a new low as even standardized test preparation guides descend into delusional polemics.

The seventh edition of Barron's *AP European History* study guide—which touts itself as the "Students' #1 Choice" and promises "everything you need" to get a top score on the AP exam—attempts to explain the French Revolution with "a chart of the political spectrum from left to right" with supposedly analogous examples from United States politics today.

Sigh. Here we go again.

"Liberals favored slower, gradual change to make things better," but "conservatives wanted no change to governance." Radicals wanted "complete, rapid and total change in government," whereas "reactionaries wanted things to be the way they were in a previous time."

Today, "most Democrats" are "in favor of small gradual change," and "most Republicans" are simply "those against change." But of course.

Leftists are "those who want to regulate banks and corporations"—as if banks and corporations are not already subject to untold thousands of pages of state, federal and local regulations. The Tea Party is directly analogous to French royalists "in the countryside who supported the monarchy"—as if the Tea Party wants "no change to governance" and supports the existing regime in United States politics.

So far, these assertions from Barron's authors, Seth A. Roberts and James M. Eder, are predictable enough. Educators, like most journalists, tilt predominately left (you know, on the political spectrum).

Things get interesting when Messrs. Roberts and Eder show the far right as "reactionary / fascist," which they define simply as "those who want things like they used to be." Never mind the bit about fascism having something to do with dictatorial rule, absolute power over individual freedom, and prohibition of dissent. If you "want things to be like they used to be"—say, because you don't want unelected judges imposing their views by fiat or because you think market-based solutions tend to work better than top-down central economic planning—you are a fascist.

Then comes the spit-take.

Who are today's reactionary fascists? Barron's seventh edition (page 168) gives the answer: "Clarence Thomas and the KKK."

Say what?!

Justice Thomas, the second Black justice of the United States Supreme Court, wrote passionately in his autobiography, *My Grandfather's Son*, of growing up during segregation and overcoming racial discrimination. Even liberals have recognized his compelling background. During Justice Thomas's confirmation process, columnist William Raspberry quoted a friend as saying, "Given the choice between two conservatives, I'll take the one who's been called 'n----r.'"

In contrast, Barron's pairs Justice Thomas with the KKK—a violently racist criminal enterprise that "was a military force serving the interests of the Democratic party, the planter class, and all those who desired the restoration of white supremacy. It aimed to destroy the Republican party's infrastructure, undermine the Reconstruction state, reestablish control of the black labor force, and restore racial subordination in every aspect of Southern life," according to liberal Columbia University professor Eric Foner's book, *A Short History of Reconstruction.*

For their own part, Messrs. Roberts and Eder should have perused the College Board's official "*Teacher's Guide for AP European History* for help on objectivity:

— "Students need to learn how to read primary and secondary sources, and even textbooks, with the understanding that the author's viewpoint may be more subjective than objective. Teach your students ... how to evaluate the validity or bias of both primary and secondary sources."

— "Without a doubt ... bias is the most frequently missed basic core point by students ... and it is also the hardest concept for students to master."

— "Name calling, loaded language, and other kinds of rhetoric betray the author's prejudices or biases."

— "What is the author's self-interest that makes the author say the things you see in the document? Do people of certain groups usually construe issues in certain ways?"

— "It is not enough to merely say that someone was biased or prejudiced. To earn credit you must give the reader your evidence that supports your assertion that someone is biased."

Those outraged by the shoddy work and flagrant bias in the Barron's guide can look to Justice Thomas's own words for guidance: "I would confide in my grandmother about my frustration," he said. "She would give me her usual sage, warm advice: 'Son, do your best, be good, be honest, and say your prayers.' I would respond, 'Yes, Ma'am!' Perhaps we all should say, 'Yes, Ma'am!' to her wise counsel and get on with the business of acting like we deserve to live in a free society."

The absolute worst I have ever been treated, the worst things that have been done to me, the worst things that have been said about me, are by northern liberal elites, not by the people of Savannah, Georgia.

Justice Clarence Thomas

CHAPTER TWENTY

Leftist Educator Can't Recover after Mask Slips

YOUR BIAS IS (STILL) SHOWING

Supreme Court Justice Clarence Thomas emerged victorious when Barron's, the test prep publisher, apologized for a diagram in its *AP European History* book that paired Justice Thomas with the Ku Klux Klan and attempted to smear him as "reactionary and/or fascist."

After I broke the story, the Twittersphere exploded and news outlets picked up the story. Eventually, Barron's responded with this sniveling, mealymouthed *mea culpa*:

> *It has been brought to our attention that Barron's* AP European History, *7th Edition by Seth Roberts and James Eder contains erroneous information that casts aspersions on Supreme Court Justice Clarence Thomas.*
>
> *In an attempt to draw a comparison between current-day politics in the US and the French National Assembly during the French Revolution, the diagram on page 168 equates Clarence Thomas with the KKK, while labeling him*

> *as a "reactionary and/or fascist." This was an unintentional error on the part of the authors and Barron's for which we sincerely apologize. By way of an explanation, in the course of formatting the book, the diagram was condensed to fit on a single page. In doing so, some information was dropped and other information was combined, which changed the original meaning of the diagram....*
>
> *It was never our intention to malign Justice Thomas, nor to become embroiled in the right vs. left politics of the day.*

Public outrage led to condemnation of the book on Amazon.com via dozens of one-star reviews. Many of the unfavorable reviews generated a comment posted by "Seth," purportedly none other than Seth Roberts, the lead author of the offending publication:

> *As the author, I would like to apologize for the political spectrum chart that appears on page 168 of the 7th edition of my book, Barron's* AP European History. *I would also like to thank those who brought it to Barron's attention, as we are always trying to find ways to improve our books. Barron's has informed me that the entire inventory of current books containing this chart is being destroyed, and all subsequent editions of the book will have the chart omitted. It was never the intention of the author or the publisher for the chart to appear the way that it did in the book.*
>
> *The chart in question was meant to help students understand the different uses of the same terms for their exam. However, the published chart contains serious editorial errors that interfere with student comprehension. I sincerely*

> *apologize for the perceived and unintentional bias that can be inferred from mistakes I failed to catch.*

It's unclear whether "Seth" is indeed the author, as he claims. However, in 2011, Seth did write a five-star Amazon.com review of the *AP European History* guide extolling its "really good" charts, "perfect" content and absence of "superfluous and pedantic detail":

> *The charts at the end of each chapter are really good... historical content is perfect... contains what students need to know for the exam without superfluous and pedantic detail.*

In any case, the statements by Barron's and "Seth" about the "unintentional" editorial errors—or "formatting" problems?—resembled the old gag from *Frasier*:

> *Say, a funny thing happened the other day. One of my patients had a rather amusing Freudian slip. He was having dinner with his wife and he meant to say, "Pass the salt." But instead he said, "You've ruined my life, you blood-sucking shrew."*

Moreover, the apologies go on and on. Their lengthy insistence—"never our intention to malign Justice Thomas, nor to become embroiled in the right vs. left politics of the day" and "sincerely apologize for the perceived and unintentional bias that can be inferred"—recalls the old Monty Python gag:

> *We would like to apologize for the way in which politicians are represented in this programme. It was never our intention to imply that politicians are weak-kneed, political*

> *time-servers who are more concerned with their personal vendettas and private power struggles than the problems of government. Nor to suggest at any point that they sacrifice their credibility by denying free debate on vital matters in the mistaken impression that party unity comes before the well-being of the people they supposedly represent. Nor to imply at any stage that they are squabbling little toadies without an ounce of concern for the vital social problems of today. Nor indeed do we intend that viewers should consider them as crabby, ulcerous, little self-seeking vermin with furry legs and an excessive addiction to alcohol and certain explicit sexual practices which some people might find offensive. We are sorry if this impression has come across.*

The self-refuting statements by Barron's and "Seth," as they attempt to defend the indefensible, reveal the true nature of the "unintentional error" behind a slur against a sitting Supreme Court justice.

CHAPTER TWENTY-ONE

Toward Sanity in Tax Policy

STOP THE TAX EXODUS

As he grew rich he grew greedy; and thinking to get at once all the gold the goose could give, he killed it and opened it only to find . . . nothing.

— Aesop

At one point, our nation's corporate tax policy reached such a point of disrepair that pundits began invoking taxpayers' patriotism to reverse an exodus overseas by corporate America. Instead, Congress should lower effective tax rates so the US can compete in the global economy and to incentivize companies to stay at home.

In recent years, American corporations have found a new tax-planning strategy: voting with their feet. Some of the largest US companies are moving offshore like so many retired New Yorkers finding tax shelter in Florida residency.

This trend has increased with US corporate taxes at a marginal rate of 35 percent and an average effective rate as high as 29 percent. American companies looking to lower their tax bills and increase their profitability are moving their tax domiciles offshore. Some big names are in play, including iconic companies like Pfizer and Walgreens.

Moving offshore for tax purposes is possible through a transaction, called an inversion, in which a US company merges with a non-US company and the combined company changes its tax home to the country offering a more efficient tax structure.

The newly offshore company can continue to do business in the US, but can slash its marginal corporate tax rate by half or even two-thirds. Companies that do so increase their ability to pay higher dividends or invest the savings back into future growth of their businesses.

"It's true that the official corporate tax rate of 39.1 percent, including state and local taxes, is the highest among members of the Organization for Economic Cooperation and Development," conceded former labor secretary Robert Reich. He was quick to point out that the effective rate after deductions, credits, "and other maneuvers" is "far lower"—but not low enough to compete with much more favorable tax rates in a place like Ireland, where the corporate tax rate is 12.5 percent.

No patriotic American wants US companies to become foreign companies. But at a certain point, a tax inversion can offer scale and efficiencies that are too attractive to overlook for companies seeking to maintain their global competitiveness.

Fortune magazine's Allan Sloan proposed a not-so-modest answer: "Fight to fix the tax code, but don't desert the country." Yet no one begrudges Aunt Bertha and Uncle Harvey for moving from New York to Florida, nor would you suggest they should dedicate their retirement to tax reform in their home state. A dose of realism is in order.

American companies innovate, create jobs, solve problems, cure life-threatening diseases, and invent nifty gizmos that make life better and more fun. There is no question we want them to stay onshore and to contribute to the US Treasury. But it's naive to think that the government can create powerful economic incentives for our largest and most successful corporations to move abroad, only to complain that the companies have followed the economic incentives that the government created.

We should, as Sloan suggests, fight to fix the tax code. Instead of a tax rate that drives US corporations overseas, we should lower the US corporate tax rate to allow US companies to keep their competitive footing and, with it, their ability to innovate, grow, and improve the lives of consumers.

"Greed often overreaches itself," Aesop cautioned, and that is what our corporate tax code has done. In trying to maximize tax revenue, we have made our corporate tax code so inhospitable as to send increasing numbers of our leading corporations offshore.

Still, the tax inversion phenomenon continues to outrage critics, including Reich. While disputing whether inversion transactions actually do result in a lower tax bill ("mostly rubbish," says Reich), he laments that tax inversions will cost the Treasury $4 billion over the next five years. Math is hard.

And yet the critics overlook a decades-old principle of federal tax law articulated by Judge Learned Hand: "Any one may so arrange his affairs that his taxes shall be as low as possible; he is not bound to choose that pattern which will best pay the Treasury; there is not even a patriotic duty to increase one's taxes."

Sloan calls inversions "positively un-American" without pausing to consider the un-American state of affairs that brought us to that place.

It's un-American to have the highest corporate tax rate among developed nations. It's un-American to create incentives that drive US companies offshore. It's un-American to impose high repatriation taxes that keep over a trillion dollars overseas and inaccessible to US job creation, innovation, and investment.

In a global economy with cross-border mergers and acquisitions, national governments compete for corporate taxpayers. Our nation simply cannot afford to impose the highest corporate taxes in the developed world. In any case, policymakers should not be surprised to see the natural effects of the economic incentives they have created as US corporations continue to migrate overseas.

CHAPTER TWENTY-TWO

Put the Death Tax

SIX FEET UNDER

Once upon a time, fiscal conservatives advocated a strategy known as "starve the beast." The theory was that cutting taxes represents the best, perhaps the only, way to check rampant government spending.

The beast is the redistributive welfare state. Conservatives advocated starvation as the only credible means of counteracting the beast's tendency to decrease the rewards of work and increase the benefits of loafing.

How quaint that all seems today. Now, instead of a weight-loss diet, the beast has its own government-sponsored ad campaign shilling for food.

Forget "starve the beast." Today's campaign brazenly demands that we "feed the pig." The taxpayer-supported Ad Council and the American Institute of Certified Public Accountants have teamed up to "encourage and help Americans aged 25 to 34 to take control of their personal finances."

This unabashedly pro-pork campaign promises to "help you think through your spending and saving habits, identify ways you can start saving and commit to making changes that will reduce your debt and grow your savings."

Here's another idea to reduce debt and grow savings: Stop spending citizens' tax dollars on ad campaigns telling them to spend less money. We promise not to waste our money on self-defeating ad campaigns.

"Feed the pig" aptly describes the federal government's estate tax regime. When you die, the federal government will take your money and spend it on advertisements encouraging you to save more.

Even more insulting than the death tax itself is its supporters' claim that it is necessary to reduce the budget deficit.

But let's face it, the death tax has nothing to do with raising revenue. Federal gift and estate taxes represent less than 0.4 percent of total federal receipts.

So why have a death tax at all? When it comes right down to it, the tax is about social engineering and confiscatory wealth redistribution.

Death-tax proponents support confiscatory taxation of lifetime earnings in the interest of wealth redistribution. And what's not to like about wealth redistribution? As Barack Obama told Joe the Plumber, "When you spread the wealth around, it's good for everybody."

Everybody? In the short run, it's certainly not good for the person whose property is taken away. Nor is it good for that person's heirs. And, in the long run, it's not good to reduce the rewards of hard work and increase the benefits of idleness, which is exactly what happens "when you spread the wealth around."

In any case, since when is it fair to take one person's rightful property and give it to someone else? "If someone builds something, it belongs to him, not the government," says economist Kevin Hassett, whereas "an entitled government undermines liberty."

Even so, the super-wealthy don't mind the idea of wealth redistribution. They have already accumulated more than they and their survivors can spend in several lifetimes. Thus, Warren Buffett and his billionaire cronies lobby Congress to keep the death tax while embracing sophisticated tax shelters available only to the super-rich.

Buffett and Bill Gates dreamed up the "giving pledge" to encourage other mega-rich plutocrats to promise to give away at least half of their wealth "to philanthropy" during their lifetimes or at death.

Buffett concedes that his apparent magnanimity involved no personal sacrifice—unlike ordinary people, who "regularly contribute to churches, schools, and other organizations," relinquishing "funds that would otherwise benefit their own families," meaning "forgone movies, dinners out, or other personal pleasures."

Buffett signed the pledge voluntarily and "will give up nothing" as a result. Yet he thinks the government should increase taxes on those who already give to charities in amounts that require forgoing movies, dinners out, and other creature comforts that billionaires will never lack.

So, if he loves taxes so much, why didn't he give the money to the federal government? Buffett's answer is that his charity does a better job at allocating resources. He says his charitable foundations "do a better job with lower administrative costs and better selection of beneficiaries than the government."

You can say that again. So why exactly does he advocate tax increases that will take more money from private-sector organizations that "do a better job than the government"? The estate tax, like the giving pledge, causes the mega-rich to give up nothing that they need or want.

For those citizens who don't hire advisors to help with sophisticated tax planning, a confiscatory death tax regime encourages them to dissipate their wealth on high living, reduced savings, earlier retirement, and less investment. Enjoy it while it lasts, before the government takes it all.

Meanwhile, the merely-rich or almost-rich need only hire lawyers, insurance agents, and accountants to structure their financial affairs in ways that avoid a whopping tax bill. Just pay a few thousand dollars in advisory fees, insurance premiums, and commissions, and you avoid millions of dollars in taxes you would otherwise pay.

For the professional advisors, it's good work if you can get it. But the underlying legal policy of the death tax makes little to no sense.

This crazy-quilt of laws and regulations, with its dubious policy objectives and paternalistic advocates who can afford to opt out of the system, exists all for the sake of collecting less than 0.4 percent of total federal tax receipts.

As Warren Buffett would say—at least when his own money is at issue—the private sector would "do a better job with lower administrative costs and better selection of beneficiaries than the government."

Time to put the death tax where it belongs: six feet under.

CHAPTER TWENTY-THREE

Lies, Damned Lies, and Tax Policy

THREE LIES

President Obama's alma mater features a well-known monument nicknamed the Statue of Three Lies. The statue's inscription reads, "John Harvard, Founder, 1638."

Clever tour guides are quick to explain. First, the man depicted in the statue is not John Harvard but Sherman Hoar of the Class of 1882. Second, John Harvard did not found the university that bears his name. Third, Harvard University was founded in 1636, not 1638.

Other than that, the statue's inscription is accurate.

For the better part of 2012—or the worse part, depending on your perspective—President Obama has touted the idea of "asking the wealthy to pay a little more." Like the statue's inscription, Obama's slogan is a monumental misrepresentation. Times three.

If Obama gets his way, the federal tax code will become a statute of three lies.

Lie number one: "ask." The government does not merely ask for taxes.

Last year, when a group of self-described "patriotic millionaires" stormed Capitol Hill to lobby for increased taxes, a reporter suggested that they use the Treasury Department's online donation page, which solicits "donations to help reduce the public debt."

Using an iPad, the reporter gave each of these high-minded plutocrats the immediate opportunity to put his money where his mouth was. All flatly refused.

"Taxes are not charity," said one in exasperation. "They are not voluntary."

You can say that again. The IRS reported almost 15,000 criminal investigations in the past three years, with almost 7,000 convictions, most resulting in jail time.

Fat-cat advocates of tax hikes already refused to give the Treasury a red cent when asked. When the federal tax code "asks" with the force of law, those who decline the invitation will receive a government-issued orange jumpsuit. Not everyone can cry poor mouth to Charlie Sheen and have him pay their taxes.

Lie number two: "the wealthy." In fact, the Obama tax increases will hit hardest our small business owners—job creators who are the lifeblood of our economy. Even the largest multinational businesses began as ideas in entrepreneurs' minds.

Warren Buffett and his crowd have already amassed their billions and can easily pay whatever chump change the government wants. You would think Buffett would gladly do that, incidentally, though he apparently enjoys flying private but doesn't see fit for his company to pay the taxes the government wants it to pay.

Lie number three: "a little more." In fact, those subject to the new Obama taxes will pay much more in new taxes.

An Ernst & Young study found that Obama's tax policy would result in a $200 billion drop in long-term economic output, 710,000 fewer jobs, lower levels of investment, a drop in real wages, and a decreased standard of living for American workers.

In practice, "a little more" translates to "it's never enough." Big-government programs are insatiable. When $833 billion of so-called "stimulus" fails, the only possible conclusion is that not enough was spent. The more you spend, the more free stuff everybody gets!

If and when the Obama tax increase fails to pay down the debt and stimulate the economy, that will only serve to prove that the tax increase was too small. Pay no attention to the giant sucking sound.

Enough already. Our aim should be to decrease the size, scope, and power of the federal government.

Obama claimed that his top priorities are jobs and growth. His tax policy of three lies ensures we will get neither.

Genius is 1% inspiration and 99% perspiration.

Thomas Edison

CHAPTER TWENTY-FOUR

Travelogue

DATELINE: CAIRO

After many years at the epicenter of revolution and cultural struggle, Cairo may find itself the locus of exciting technological developments. Today's Cairo is a hotbed not of political strife, but of entrepreneurship and innovation.

RiseUp15, recently held in Cairo, brought together the Middle East's leading entrepreneurs, global investors, and learners of all ages and backgrounds. The annual summit occurs on the downtown GrEEK Campus, not far from Tahrir Square, where iconic protests unfolded before a watchful world during the 2011 pro-democracy uprisings then known as the Arab Spring.

A lifelong interest in ancient Egypt led me to visit Cairo to experience the mystery and wonder of this city in person. As my plane touched down, my cellphone lit up with texts and email alerts warning, after the fact, of a bombing at the Italian consulate just hours earlier.

Traveling by car to my first destination, I began to absorb the sights and sounds of the place Egyptians call Umm ad-Dunya, the "Mother of the World." Many mothers of this world first caught my eye as they boldly carried their infants across four-lane highways with cars speeding in both directions, a harrowing real-life version of the decades-old classic video game *Frogger*, whose object is to cross a busy multilane highway without going splat.

A local informed me that Cairo's lack of traffic laws or enforcement shows that Egypt is more democratic than the United States: People are not hemmed in by restrictive laws or policing.

As the nerve-wracking excitement subsided, the mechanical dance of Egyptian traffic and the back-and-forth of driver and pedestrian took on an orderly and strangely efficient feel. In contrast to notoriously aggressive and gridlocked traffic back in Washington, the Cairo traffic maintained a constant motion in which everyone seemed to know his or her place.

Check-in procedures at a Western hotel chain seemed typical other than airport-style security screening, for which I walked through a metal detector and they X-rayed my luggage. Having made the trip from Giza to downtown Cairo, I was eager to meet with local entrepreneurs and experience local culture.

My first stop was at the GrEEK Campus, the brainchild of Los Angeles-based Egyptian-American entrepreneur Ahmed Alfi. Alfi spent two decades investing in technology and media, and he returned to Cairo to start one of the earliest Egyptian venture capital funds, Sawari Ventures. Ahmed started the technology start-up accelerator Flat6Labs in addition to the GrEEK Campus.

The GrEEK Campus comprises five large buildings with classrooms, a library, offices, and sweeping staircases. A grassy courtyard in the center holds eye-catching modern art, including a sculpture of a dinosaur chewing on an old computer keyboard and colorful sculptures of ancient Egyptian pharaohs scrambling up the tall walls, giving a nod to the past and making a statement about the present.

Diverse types populate the GrEEK Campus, from undergraduate and graduate students with a burning idea to share with the world, to twenty-somethings who have launched an idea or two but hunger for more, to experienced entrepreneurs who mentor the up-and-comers while looking for new investment opportunities.

All of them meet at the ping-pong table in the courtyard for friendly competition, new relationships, and prospective opportunities.

The animating ideas vary widely: a babysitting service for upper-class families who need occasional help and value the care college or graduate students can provide their children; a reliable car-repair service that will schedule appointments with reputable garages; an advanced software-based pen to improve classroom learning.

Some ideas target eventual profit, whereas others target socially oriented goals centered on solutions for providing an underserved populace with food, water, energy, health care, and education.

Defying stereotypes of Islamic women's roles in the Middle East, the most impressive of the dozens of entrepreneurs I met were women. At the GrEEK Campus, Sally Halawa sat with me in the studio of Kemet Art and Design, sharing with me her vision to bring design skills to young Egyptians. Halawa exudes grace and refinement. Having previously worked at the Egyptian Museum, her passion is to open the world of design to others.

Hanan Abdel Meguid, a woman with sleek, curly black hair and a friendly smile, founded Kamelizer, an angel investment fund focused on technology start-ups. An experienced businesswoman, Meguid sees the values of investing and supporting young Egyptian companies as they build products and assess market potential. Kamelizer's role is to take a company from seed-capital stage to an early institutional financing round. Her young assistants brimmed with enthusiasm, creativity, and determination.

Across town, Alfi's other initiative, Flat6Labs, resides in a nondescript building on a narrow street. Alfi and many others like him are profiled in Christopher Schroeder's *Startup Rising: The Entrepreneurial*

Revolution Remaking the Middle East, an intriguing book describing how technology promises to transform the Middle East.

At Flat6Labs, entrepreneurs submit their plans for review on a quarterly cycle. Each quarter, Flat6Labs receives upwards of 400 online applications, of which roughly sixty applicants gain interviews. Experts pare the sixty down to ten start-ups that receive four months of intensive training and support. For these finalists, Flat6Labs incubates them with seed funding, office space, computers, Internet access, training, legal support, and tax advice while nurturing an ecosystem to provide continuing support for its graduates.

There, I met Dana Khater. At nineteen years old, Khater became Flat6Labs' youngest entrepreneur. She applied to the cycle on a whim, just four hours before the deadline. Despite having no business partner, which usually leads to rejection, she was accepted. While dreaming up her fashion business, she studied electrical engineering and economics at the American University in Cairo (AUC), often the only woman in her class and frequently hearing that she was in the wrong class. Most of the women, Khater explained, transferred to the business classes.

Khater started a cupcake business at age fifteen and, while a college student, produced the AUC fashion magazine after rejection from a school-sponsored initiative led her mother to encourage her to start a magazine on her own.

Through Flat6Labs, Khater launched Coterique. Her first customer, based in Los Angeles, found her online. Her second customer came from New York City. She had to buck the cultural expectation of the traditional career track of college, then a steady corporate job for a well-known company like Procter & Gamble, where she could climb the corporate ladder.

Khater senses a change. More people now think it's cool that she is running a start-up. To would-be female entrepreneurs, she gives ready advice: "Start young and just do it! Though it is not cool to be broke and struggling, it is okay to keep struggling."

Coterique has experienced steady monthly growth, with sales to international celebrities including a well-known Hollywood actress, the wife of a Real Madrid player, and the head designer at a major apparel brand. Her company is now in a $1.5 million financing round to raise money to hire top talent and fuel future growth in the Middle East and Asia.

These three female entrepreneurs share a common bond with their Western counterparts. They want to improve their communities, serve others, and create value. And they do this despite the challenges and changes of a complex and dynamic world. The promise of Cairo's future does not require it to become the next Silicon Valley. In a city known as the Mother of the World, women are turning challenges into opportunities.

Above all, we must realize that no arsenal, or no weapon in the arsenals of the world, is so formidable as the will and moral courage of free men and women. It is a weapon our adversaries in today's world do not have.

President Ronald Reagan

CHAPTER TWENTY-FIVE

Time to Move On from the Obama Years

FREE AT LAST

With domestic and world affairs in shambles, it is high time for President Obama to do the wave, get on the helicopter, and leave the White House for good. In areas as diverse as foreign policy, national security, our economy, the trustworthiness of our federal agencies, so-called "women's issues," executive power, and religious liberty, the president and his hapless minions have taken us to a new low.

Mr. Obama set the course for his Middle East policy in his Cairo speech of June 2009. He promised to withdraw all US troops by August 2010 and to "leave Iraq to the Iraqis" and would later compare the Islamic State of Iraq and Syria (ISIS) to a "JV team." But, as a result of his withdrawal of our troops in 2011, we have instead left Iraq to ISIS, a group whose brutality now makes Afghanistan's Taliban and 9/11's al-Qaeda themselves look like JV teams.

ISIS routinely beheads children, throws gay men off tall buildings, sells women into sexual slavery, and destroys priceless global cultural heritage like ancient Palmyra. Reflecting on US power, Mr. Obama once quoted Thomas Jefferson's hope "that our wisdom will grow with our power, and teach us that the less we use our power the greater it will be." Mr. Obama could not use less power abroad if he tried. Is American power greater as a result?

Take a short tour around the rest of the region: Libya, Yemen, Syria, Nigeria, and Tunisia have seen the collapse of governments, devastating civil wars, and horrific terrorist attacks on innocent civilians.

"To those who cling to power through corruption and deceit and the silencing of dissent, know that you are on the wrong side of history," Obama pointedly said upon taking office, "but that we will extend a hand if you are willing to unclench your fist." Every day since, the corrupt, deceitful, and intolerant regime of the Islamic Republic of Iran has continued to raise its tightly clenched fist and shout "Death to America!"

The Iranian regime has benefitted from Mr. Obama's insistence on ramming through Congress his dangerous nuclear deal. After repeating for twenty-four months the mantra, "No deal is better than a bad deal," the administration has abruptly switched to "No deal equals war."

The capitulation gives Iran carte blanche toward its nuclear ambitions and guarantees an economic windfall of $150 billion for the same Iranian regime that violently suppressed political dissent during the Green Revolution of 2009 and unabashedly holds four Americans in its deplorable prisons.

The administration's foreign policy has produced failure at every turn. A promised reset of relations with Russia resulted only in the Russian takeover of Crimea and ongoing fighting in Ukraine. Listless relations with China have stoked Chinese aggression in the Southeast Asian region, worrying our allies and emboldening our enemies.

At home, Mr. Obama took office promising to improve our economy by increasing taxes, creating more central-planning government mandates from Washington apparatchiks, enlarging government aid, and creating "shovel-ready jobs."

Americans receiving food stamps now number 45 million, of which 13.2 million are new food stamp recipients, and the poverty rate has only increased. Not since 1977 has our labor participation rate been so low.

Median income has declined and family health care premiums have increased by $4,154 per year, despite the president's promises of lower costs. New regulations since Obama took office handcuff our economy and cost an estimated $95 billion per year, despite the president's promises to reduce bureaucratic red tape.

No sober-minded observer believed the soaring rhetoric at the time. For those who did, the current reality has awakened them.

You might think that with the increase in federal government handouts, the popular perception of government would improve. Yet, when the IRS became weaponized against conservative groups, the danger of centralized power again became too obvious to ignore.

Women in particular have fared poorly in the Obama years, continuing to lose ground in his economy as negative or slow job growth has had a disparate impact on women. Food stamp recipients outnumber the women who work full time.

Despite the administration's wage-gap rhetoric, women in Obama's White House earn only 88 cents for each dollar paid to men. Last year, only 30 percent of female employees in the administration made the top salary of $172,000. Women are paid at the lower end of the pay scale across all parts of the same federal government that would seek to regulate private-sector wages.

Our health care system has become less affordable without any increase in quality of care. Families have lost their preferred plans despite the president's countless promises that "if you like your plan you can keep it."

The same president who infamously insisted "I am not a dictator" has issued dozens of executive orders codifying lawless fiats that overreach into wide-ranging areas of federal law from immigration to religious liberty.

Toward the end of the Bush presidency, an inside-the-Beltway bumper sticker declared, "1.20.09: The End of an Error." Now, in the twilight of the Obama presidency, we see clearly that Inauguration Day 2017 will mark the end of errors too numerous to count.

CHAPTER TWENTY-SIX

The Extraordinary Temar Boggs

AMERICAN HERO

On an ordinary summer afternoon in Lancaster, Pennsylvania, five-year-old Jocelyn Rojas entertained herself playing in her grandmother's front yard. With blonde hair, brown eyes, stylish glasses, and a courageous, radiant smile, Jocelyn was the picture of an adorable all-American girl.

A white man in his seventies approached her. He walked with a limp. Witnesses say he wore green shoes, green pants, and a red-and-white striped shirt.

Preying on her innocence, he persuaded Jocelyn to accompany him. He offered to buy her some ice cream. She trusted him.

And just like that, they both vanished.

Jocelyn's family called the police. Authorities issued an Amber Alert signaling a serious child-abduction case.

"Horrible, horrible thoughts flashed through my mind," said Jocelyn's grandmother.

Monsters exist. In real life, they are much scarier than the imaginary horrors of science fiction.

Each year, low-life scumbags abduct about 58,000 unrelated children, primarily for sexual purposes, according to the National Center for Missing and Exploited Children. Nearly half of these children are sexually assaulted.

Far too often, the abductors murder the children, hold them for ransom, or intend to keep them indefinitely.

"You see the Amber Alerts and you think, 'I feel for that family,'" said Jocelyn's grandmother. "But when you're in that situation ... it's horrible."

The Amber Alert galvanized the community. People of all ages joined in the search for Jocelyn.

Temar Boggs, a fifteen-year-old African American, was helping move an elderly woman's couch at a nearby apartment complex that evening when he learned of the ongoing search.

He and his friend Chris Garcia hopped on their bikes. About a half-mile from the apartment complex, Boggs spotted Jocelyn in a dark red car with an old White man behind the wheel.

Boggs knew they had little time to prevent a young child from becoming another heartbreaking story on the evening news.

He was not going to let that happen. The young men spotted Jocelyn and pursued the car for fifteen minutes.

"Every time we would go down the street, he would turn back around, and we'd go back and follow him," Boggs told WGAL.

"As soon as the guy started noticing that we were chasing him, he stopped at the end of the hill and let her out," Boggs recalled. "She ran to me and said that she needed her mom."

Boggs realizes that he might have saved Jocelyn's life. He sees it as "a blessing for me to make that happen." His proud mother remarked that Boggs is "learning what I tell him, to help others."

Without regard for his own personal safety, fifteen-year-old Temar Boggs "distinguished himself conspicuously by gallantry and intrepidity at the risk of his life above and beyond the call of duty."

Soldiers who meet that standard receive the Congressional Medal of Honor. Boggs deserves similar recognition for his valor.

One little girl and her family will never forget that monsters lurk among us, seeking to do us harm, and heroes take the shape of a fearless fifteen-year-old African American boy on a bike.

In the polarized aftermath of the George Zimmerman trial, we should recognize and celebrate the ones who make our country great, of any age or race.

Let's make Temar Boggs a household name and teach our children what it means to be a hero.

Our country, our people, and our laws have to be our top priority.

PRESIDENT DONALD J. TRUMP

CHAPTER TWENTY-SEVEN

Pandemic Press Conferences Show Desperately Biased Media

NO MATCH FOR TRUMP

Millions of people worldwide are watching President Donald Trump's frequent press conferences on the global pandemic. (Better ratings than *The Bachelor!* Maybe better ratings than *Monday Night Football!*)

There are two striking things about these press conferences. The first is what they reveal about the media, and the second is what they show about Mr. Trump.

On the first point, the interactions between the president and the press show that the craven, absurdly biased, anti-Trump, pro-China media corps still have not changed their approach, despite an ongoing global crisis and their repeated efforts to cause him to fail.

The media corps have doubled and tripled down on their attacks against the Trump administration. There is no spirit of unity that pervaded the post-9/11 atmosphere. No coming together of national interest in the face of a modern-day plague.

A new strain of biased reporting has emerged: "Live TV enables the President to lie to Americans about Covid-19," says *The Washington Post*. Add to that a new mutation of lazy coverage: "Save time: Assume Trump is inept and lying."

This is no surprise from the newspaper that publishes a rolling catalogue of so-called "lies" supposedly told by the president. "President Trump made 16,241 false or misleading claims in his first three years"! A fictional number, but more manageable than tabulating the false or misleading claims of *The Washington Post* or the general phenomenon of "opinion journalism pretending to some sort of heightened objectivity," as James Taranto has repeatedly said.

On and on it goes. *The New York Times*: "Google gives cover to Trump's lies." *The Atlantic*: "Trump's blatant coronavirus lies." *The Daily Beast*: "Trump's coronavirus lies are an infection. This is the only cure" (suggesting "doses of truth").

Here's another representative headline: "Broadcasting Trump's Coronavirus Briefings Live Is a Danger to Public Health." A new twist? Not even close. This one is as old as his time in office: "President Donald Trump Is a Threat to Public Health," claimed the *Harvard Public Health Review* in 2017. "The first task of the doctor is political," said the laughably unmedical argument. "The struggle against disease must begin with a war against bad government." (Nothing about undercooked bat meat.)

And, while corporate media attack Mr. Trump and brand him a liar, they uncritically republish Chinese communist propaganda in a manner reminiscent of *Pravda's* dissemination of USSR disinformation.

Lacking professional skepticism, and despite early evidence that the Chinese government covered up the catastrophe as it unfolded in Wuhan unimpeded while brave Chinese health experts risked their lives to spread the truth, the China-credulous media continue to parrot the Chinese government's official reports. Some of the US media's coverage even praised the Chinese government for "helping Italy" in its fight against the virus.

With all of these forces arrayed against the president, a fair-minded observer might wonder if this is a fair fight. It's not.

And that leads me to my second observation about the press conferences. Mr. Trump is winning.

The colloquies between Mr. Trump and media showcase his mastery of the press conference format and, let's face it, complete dominance over his adversaries known as White House media correspondents. The press conferences succeed so well that Mr. Trump's adversaries in the media even want to stop live broadcasting and straight-news reporting during a pandemic.

Once again Mr. Trump is disrupting the media narrative. Even with his campaign rallies cancelled and most Americans unable to engage in their regular daily lives, the president's disruptive ability as a communicator harken back to his 2016 presidential campaign, when virtually all forces of the mainstream media were unable to stop the steam-locomotive power of the Trump Train.

The press briefings are yet another medium in which Mr. Trump can speak directly and unfiltered to voters. Viewers who tune in and watch the briefings live can see firsthand Mr. Trump's mastery of the process. Media mendacity cannot stop him. Even with journalists' misleading snippets and their spliced-together fragments designed to deceive or isolate words from context, the president continues to win.

When a reporter tried to ambush Mr. Trump with a selectively misleading quote from an earlier press conference, the president forced the reporter to admit on live television that he had omitted the sentences in which Mr. Trump praised his team and the Army Corps of Engineers.

As a Bloomberg reporter readied an attempt at a gotcha question, Mr. Trump asked, "How's Michael doing? Good?" as the audience chuckled.

In a defining moment, and my own personal favorite, another reporter asked, "How many deaths are acceptable?" to which the president immediately responded, "How many deaths are acceptable to me? None. Okay? None, if that's your question."

To this gotcha question designed to elicit a gaffe, the president delivered a knockout punch. No deaths are acceptable. Pure and simple. The media continue to try to trip up the president during these press briefings. Having repeatedly failed, they now want to shut down live coverage.

The pandemic has not changed the mainstream media's war against Mr. Trump. As much as they try to leverage our current crisis to debilitate the president, their efforts continue to backfire.

CHAPTER TWENTY-EIGHT

Amish Case Shows Limits of Religious Exemption

VACCINE MANDATES

New mandates could force millions of Americans to get the coronavirus vaccine. But exemptions may be available for those who have a medical condition or a sincerely held religious belief that prevents them from getting vaccinated. In our world of bureaucrats gone wild, what counts as a "sincerely held religious belief" is anything but simple.

A recent case, unrelated to the pandemic, illustrates the point. When an Amish community in Minnesota sought a religious exemption from state water control regulations, power-hungry bureaucrats denied the religious exemption, claiming that the group's religious beliefs were not sincerely held.

The Amish don't live like most Americans. They deliberately lack the modern conveniences we enjoy. Our pop culture celebrates the unshakable Amish fidelity to their cherished beliefs. Anyone knows that from the movie *Witness*, starring Harrison Ford, Weird Al Yankovic's satirical "Amish Paradise" (a send-up of Coolio's non-Amish "Gangsta's Paradise") or the reality show *Breaking Amish*.

When the Minnesota Pollution Control Agency (MPCA) targeted one of the most traditional Amish communities for failing to comply with a water treatment mandate, it threatened to displace the Amish from their homes, move all their possessions, and declare their homes uninhabitable if they did not comply. Far from fighting homelessness, the MPCA tried hard to cause it.

Our nation is founded on principles of religious toleration and free exercise of religion. Our Bill of Rights protects these individual rights, and Congress has enacted statutes to strengthen these protections.

Generally applicable laws and regulations may not govern where they intrude or burden the free exercise of religion. We see the point in a *Dilbert* comic about jury selection. A potential juror tells the judge, "Your honor, it is against my religion to judge others. Only God may judge." The judge excuses the juror. Another potential juror, noticing how easily the first candidate was excused, exclaims, "Ooh ooh! I just changed my religion!"

In his commentary, *Dilbert* creator Scott Adams asks, "Is there any rule that says how long you need to be in a religion?" If so, the Amish would certainly qualify. They trace their origins to a group in Switzerland more than 300 years ago.

The Amish community at the center of this fight is one of the most traditional Amish groups, the Swartzentruber Amish. Swartzentruber Amish don't use electricity or cars. They don't use mechanical refrigeration. They don't have running water for bathtubs or indoor flush toilets or chain saws. They dress in heavy, plain clothes that cover down to their shoes. You will never see a Swartzentruber Amish riding a bicycle or even using Velcro.

In response, the Amish tried to work with the system and offered alternatives to comply with the state water controls. The bureaucrats responded by seeking a court order "authorizing its agents to inspect the inside of Amish homes as part of an 'investigation' into what 'types of modern technologies and materials' they might be using" to collect evidence that the Amish's religious beliefs might be insincerely held.

The county bureaucrats did not stop there. They tried to argue that the "Bible commands the Amish to submit to secular authority," so of course the Amish don't understand their own religion and should give in to the county's interpretation of the Amish faith.

After losing in the lower courts, the Amish took their case to the United States Supreme Court. The Supreme Court vacated the lower court decision and sent the case back to the lower courts for further proceedings.

Justice Neil Gorsuch issued an opinion concurring with the Supreme Court's order. He eloquently explained that the lower court must apply strict scrutiny, meaning the government must prove that the county regulation serves a compelling governmental interest and that the regulation is narrowly tailored to serve that interest.

The Amish had requested an exemption from the county that would accomplish the goal of the regulation and yet preserve their observance of their faith. Gorsuch called out the county, noting the many exemptions already given under the regulation, including exemptions for hunters and fishers.

Why was this same flexibility not granted to the Amish? Other states also allow the solution proposed by the Amish. Why the double standard and inflexibility of the county when it should be giving even more latitude based on the governing statute protecting religious freedom?

Despite some disappointing decisions on free exercise during the beginning of the COVID-19 disruptions, the current majority of the Supreme Court respects the value of religious liberty. "In this country," said Gorsuch, "neither the Amish nor anyone else should have to choose between their farms and their faith."

That is a truth as plain as the clothing of the Swartzentruber Amish. Yet they were forced to spend years in litigation to protect their beliefs. Even now, their fight may be far from over, as their litigation continues.

Your freedoms may depend on a bureaucrat's discretion to decide whether your religious beliefs are sincere. Power-hungry bureaucrats do crazy things such as claiming that beer is essential but Easter is not or that the Amish are not sincere in their beliefs.

Ultimately, that does not bode well for Americans hoping to demonstrate a sincerely held religious objection to vaccination.

CHAPTER TWENTY-NINE

Government of the Experts?

NO THANK YOU, DR. FAUCI

In the midst of our greatest national struggle, Abraham Lincoln called upon all Americans to ensure that "government of the people, by the people and for the people shall not perish from the Earth." Who would have imagined that Honest Abe's highest aspirations could be undone by . . . a microbe?

Today, as a pandemic covers the globe, hypocritical bureaucrats impose far-reaching restrictions while barely pretending to abide by their own rules. "Trust the experts," we are told. Yet most Americans are skeptical of being governed by unelected technocrats.

We know full well the perils of government by expert and the threat it poses to our individual liberty. Expert rule is an elitist political philosophy that has rapidly metastasized during the pandemic.

The coronavirus pandemic "has resulted in previously unimaginable restrictions on individual liberty," said Justice Samuel Alito in his recent address to the Federalist Society. "We have never before seen restrictions as severe, extensive and prolonged as those experienced for most of 2020."

Restrictions proliferate as positive tests climb. New Mexico and Oregon have implemented two-week lockdowns. Chicago Mayor Lori Lightfoot issued a thirty-day stay-at-home order and proposes to cancel Thanksgiving. New York Gov. Andrew Cuomo requires bars and restaurants to close by 10 p.m. and makes traditional family and friends Thanksgiving celebrations unlawful by limiting indoor gatherings at private homes to no more than ten people. California and Washington draw a hard line against "nonessential" travel.

President-elect Joe Biden's campaign team is pushing a nationwide mask mandate to be coordinated with state governors and mayors. Biden's top COVID-19 adviser has proposed a nationwide lockdown of up to six weeks along with—what else?—a big, fat government "package to cover all lost wages, for losses to small companies to medium-sized companies, and city, state and county governments."

Of course, the very same people making these impositions on the individual rights of Americans unashamedly flaunt their own disregard for these restrictions. Lockdowns for thee but not for me.

Lightfoot celebrated in the street with thousands of Biden supporters. California Gov. Gavin Newsom was caught attending a high-end birthday celebration in violation of his own restrictions. Fancy celebrations are fine for those in power, but down-home Thanksgiving dinners for hardworking families are verboten. Trust the experts!

We could go on. House Speaker Nancy Pelosi's Marie Antoinette moment at the hair salon. Cuomo's insanely flawed policy stating, "No resident shall be denied re-admission or admission to the [nursing home] solely based on a confirmed or suspected diagnosis of COVID-19." Trust the experts!

How did we get here? "The vision of early 20th-century progressives and the New Dealers of the 1930s was that policymaking would shift from narrow-minded elected legislators to an elite group of appointed experts," said Alito. "In a word, the policymaking would become more scientific."

In the ultra-leftist suburban neighborhoods of Washington, D.C., two popular yard signs are "Thank you Dr. Fauci!" and "Science is real." (See how this works? "My political opponents are anti-science!") Meanwhile, let's remember what Dr. Fauci is telling Americans. Give up your "independent spirit" and "do what you are told." Oh, and forget about having Christmas too. Everybody gets a lump of coal in their stocking.

Fauci, like Lightfoot, Cuomo, Newsom, and Pelosi, lost public confidence after his original claim that "there's no reason to be walking around with a mask," followed by his dogged insistence on mask compliance, along with his own conspicuously unmasked face at a Washington Nationals baseball game after he attempted to throw out the first pitch.

Alito calls our attention to a long-term trend to take power out of the hands of the elected representatives and vest it in unaccountable and hypocritical experts. The pandemic crisis created an opportunity to accelerate that trend. It won't stop there: We will see it employed for gun bans, stifling religious liberty and economic policies.

"All sorts of things can be called an emergency or disaster of major proportions," said Alito. "Simply slapping on that label cannot provide the ground for abrogating our most fundamental rights."

New Jersey Gov. Phil Murphy implemented some of the harshest restrictions, and yet his state endured the worst death rate. Asked about the implications of his actions under the Bill of Rights, he responded, "That's above my pay grade."

Ultimately, "liberty lies in the hearts of men and women," as Alito reminds us. "When it dies there, no constitution, no law, no court can do much to help it."

Let freedom ring. Let us "highly resolve," as Lincoln said, that government of the people, by the people, and for the people shall not perish from the Earth. And as for government of the experts, by the experts, and for the experts: No thank you, Dr. Fauci!

www.ingramcontent.com/pod-product-compliance
Lightning Source LLC
Chambersburg PA
CBHW060239030426
42335CB00014B/1524
9798985586701